ONE AMAZING FILMMAKER AT A TIME

ENA VISMAY

Contents

Prologue: A Tribute

The marvel that is Bollywood has often been reduced to a shorthand for glamour, spectacle, and song. To many across the world, it conjures images of lovers dancing in mustard fields, of heartbreak rendered in melody, of vibrant colours cascading through frames. But Indian cinema is far more than a pop-culture genre. It is a living, evolving narrative of a subcontinent—messy, contradictory, exhilarating, profound. It holds a mirror to the nation's dreams and discontents, and in doing so, it tells the story of India in motion. Bollywood is not a place. It is a pulse.

From silent reels to streaming platforms, Indian cinema has journeyed through a hundred years of reinvention. It began quietly, with Dadasaheb Phalke's *Raja Harishchandra* in 1913, a mythological tale told without sound but not without soul. The early decades saw the rise of studios like Bombay Talkies and Prabhat Film Company, as cinema took its place among the other arts. The '40s and '50s were defined by melodrama and idealism, with the likes of Mehboob Khan and Bimal Roy framing tales of sacrifice and injustice against the backdrop of a newly independent India. The '60s brought both glamour and gravitas, with filmmakers like Raj Kapoor and Guru Dutt giving Indian cinema a global signature—one of melancholic beauty and grand emotion.

By the '70s, the era of the 'angry young man' dawned, shaped by directors like Prakash Mehra and Ramesh Sippy, who turned social frustration into blockbuster narratives. Parallel to this, the rise of 'art cinema' in the hands of Shyam Benegal, Govind Nihalani, and Adoor Gopalakrishnan offered a starker, more politically charged aesthetic. The '90s were a time of transformation—globalisation, liberalisation, and a new kind of romance. Filmmakers like Aditya Chopra, Karan Johar, and later Imtiaz Ali redefined Hindi cinema for the diaspora and multiplex generation. The twenty-first century has seen an even greater broadening of the canvas, with genre-defying filmmakers like Anurag Kashyap, Zoya Akhtar, and Sriram Raghavan blurring the lines between indie and mainstream, between mass appeal and cinematic risk.

But to call this only the story of Bollywood would be a distortion. Regional cinema has long been a cornerstone of India's filmic expression. Bengali cinema, under the stewardship of Satyajit Ray, Ritwik Ghatak, and Mrinal Sen, offered films that rivalled European arthouse in elegance and insight. Malayalam filmmakers like Adoor Gopalakrishnan and Girish Kasaravalli brought meditative realism to the fore. Tamil cinema gave us the theatrical precision of K. Balachander and the pan-Indian star-director Kamal Haasan. Marathi cinema—once the birthplace of Indian film—has seen a quiet renaissance in recent years. The list goes on: from Assamese to Kannada, from Manipuri to Punjabi, every language has contributed a distinct rhythm, rooted in place but reaching outward.

Documentary filmmaking, too, has played a crucial role in shaping India's cinematic conscience. Filmmakers like Anand Patwardhan and Deepa Dhanraj turned the camera into a tool of protest, documenting social movements, communal violence, and systemic injustice with rigour and empathy. Wildlife filmmakers like Mike Pandey and Kartiki Gonsalves reminded us of the non-human world, of elephants and vultures, of forests and coastlines, and our fragile place within them. These films may not always command box-office numbers, but their power lies in holding the gaze when others look away. This book is both a celebration and a curation. It profiles 60 iconic directors whose work has helped define Indian cinema in its many hues. Each filmmaker is a prism, refracting stories through their unique sensibilities. Some trade in opulence and operatic emotion, others deconstruct narrative itself. Some raise fists; others hold mirrors.

But the very nature of selection implies omission. For every director profiled, there are others equally deserving. Our epilogue—Beyond 60—pays a tribute to those we could not profile. This is not a definitive list. It is a guided journey.

Ultimately, India's contribution to world cinema is not just in its volume, but in its variety—the operatic and the austere, the blockbuster and the whisper. No other country makes films in as many languages, across as many aesthetic traditions, and for as many types of audiences. It is an industry, yes, but also a laboratory, a circus, a classroom, a confessional. It is where a song can stop a revolution, and a gaze can ignite one.

And today, the next generation is already reimagining the frame. Whether it's Chaitanya Tamhane's *The Disciple,* Rima Das' *Village Rockstars*, or the quietly radical work of Shuchi Talati or Devashish Makhija, young Indian filmmakers are no longer asking for a seat at the global table—they're building new ones. With digital platforms breaking barriers of language and location, and with a growing appetite for stories both hyperlocal and universal, Indian cinema stands at the threshold of a new golden age.

This book is our humble tribute to the artists who brought us here—one amazing filmmaker at a time.

FATHER OF INIDAN
CINEMA

Dadasaheb Phalke

The Father of Indian Cinema

(30 April 1870–16 February 1944)

While colonial India was in a thick swirl in the early 1900s—the Partition of Bengal, the Swadeshi Movement, Tilak's Swaraj, and a boom in vernacular newspapers and periodicals—around the world, cinema was just emerging as a new medium.

A middle-aged Maharashtrian artist from Bombay's Sir J.J. School of Art, Dhundiraj Govind Phalke, deeply into photography, printing, and the visual arts, sat watching *The Life of Christ* at the America-India Picture Palace in 1910. As scenes from Christ's life unfolded on screen, Phalke was transfixed … by the power of storytelling through moving images. Imagining Lord Rama and Krishna coming to life in a similar way, he famously said, 'I want to show our gods to our people.' That moment would mark the birth of Indian cinema.

The OG filmmaker, as we'd say today, travelled to London in 1912 to learn the craft of filmmaking. He met British film pioneer Cecil Hepworth and secured equipment and film stock. Phalke set up a small studio in his house and began work on *Raja Harishchandra,* India's first full-length feature film. Released in 1913, the mythological tale of the righteous king Harishchandra, who sacrifices everything for truth, was written, directed, produced, shot, and even processed by Phalke and became a resounding success.

Phalke did face numerous challenges—including societal resistance to cinema and the taboo of women acting in films (he famously cast a male actor, Salunke, in the role of Queen Taramati)—but he persisted, driven by his belief that cinema could be a force of cultural revival against colonialism. He made over 90 films and 26 short features, often drawing from Indian epics and folklore.

Hailed as the 'Father of Indian Cinema', Dadasaheb Phalke's vision, artistry, and pioneering zeal laid the groundwork for what's now one of the world's largest film industries. In recognition of his monumental contribution, the Government of India instituted the Dadasaheb Phalke Award in 1969, the highest honour in Indian cinema. Phalke's legacy endures, not just in awards but in the very language of Indian film … where mythology, music, and storytelling continue to inspire generations.

মানিকদা

Satyajit Ray

The Maestro with a Storyteller's Heart

(2 May 1921–23 April 1992)

If Dadasaheb Phalke birthed Indian Cinema, then Satyajit Ray became the father of Indian Art House Cinema—he gave Indian cinema its soul.

Ray's *Pather Panchali* (1955) introduced Indian cinema to the global stage, winning the Best Human Document at the 1956 Cannes Film Festival and dozens of international awards.He broke away from the dominant song-dance melodrama of Indian commercial cinema and used non-professional actors, real locations, natural light, and minimalist music to create a profoundly emotional, neorealist film, beginning the Parallel Cinema movement in India—a school of filmmaking that valued realism, depth, and subtlety over spectacle.

Manik, as he was called, was born into an illustrious Bengali family in Calcutta, entrenched in art and literature—his grandfather, Upendrakishore Ray (Roychowdhury), was a renowned writer, illustrator, and publisher, while his father, Sukumar Ray, was a pioneer of Bengali nonsense verse and children's literature. Surrounded by creativity, his imagination nurtured by stories and lively intellectual discussions, Manik briefly spent time at Santiniketan, where Tagore's humanistic philosophy deeply influenced him.

In 1950, Ray went to London for work and immersed himself in world cinema, devouring films by masters like Vittorio De Sica and Jean Renoir. De Sica's masterpiece, *Bicycle Thieves*, resonated deeply with him, solidifying his belief that powerful stories could be told with modest means. In the following three decades, Ray directed a diverse array of films, each marked by his unique style. He tackled social issues in *Devi* (1960), explored urban anxieties in *Mahanagar* (1963), and created intricate psychological dramas like *Charulata* (1964), often hailed as his masterpiece. His versatility extended to children's films, detective stories, and historical epics.

In the twilight of his life, despite ill health, Ray continued to create. His final film, *Agantuk* (1991), was a poignant reflection on tradition, modernity, and belief. In 1992, the Academy of Motion Picture Arts and Sciences bestowed upon him an honorary Academy Award for his contribution to cinema. Ray's humanism, cinematic brilliance, and legacy as a pioneer and auteur remain as luminous as the stories he so masterfully brought to life.

SATYAM SHIVAM SUNDARAM
FILMS

Raj Kapoor

The Greatest Showman of Indian Cinema

(14 December 1924–2 June 1988)

The '50s and '60s—the Golden Age of Indian Cinema—saw legendary directors like Ray, Ritwik Ghatak, and Mrinal Sen in Bengal and Guru Dutt, Raj Kapoor, and Bimal Roy in Hindi cinema.

Ranbir Raj Kapoor hailed from Indian cinema's 'First Family'—intertwined in film and theatre. The patriarch Prithviraj Kapoor founded Prithvi Theatres in 1944 and was also a founding figure of Hindi cinema through iconic films like *Alam Ara* (India's first talkie, 1931) and *Mughal-e-Azam* (1960). Raj was the eldest of six siblings. Brothers Shammi and Shashi also became major film stars, while sons Randhir, Rishi, and Rajiv became successful actors and filmmakers, too. With grandchildren Karisma, Kareena, and Ranbir as Bollywood's biggest stars today, it's an unmatched four generations of stardom in Indian cinema.

Crafting the 'Indian Everyman'—a lovable, struggling, morally upright character symbolising the aspirations, innocence, and struggles of post-independence India—Raj Kapoor created deeply Indian yet universally resonant films. *Awara* (1951) and *Shree 420* (1955) made him a superstar not only in India but across Russia, China, the Middle East, and Eastern Europe. He said half-jokingly: 'In Russia, they did not know my name—they just called me "Awara".' Inspired by Charlie Chaplin's Little Tramp, he said, 'Charlie made the world laugh at sorrow. I wanted to make the world smile at hope.' Kapoor's collaborations with Shankar-Jaikishan, Mukesh, Lata Mangeshkar, and Shailendra produced some of the greatest soundtracks in Indian history. Mukesh was often called 'Raj Kapoor's soul'.

Mera Naam Joker, his magnum opus, deeply personal, philosophical, and his greatest artistic gamble, took six years to complete, and at over four hours long, it was released in two parts on the same day in 1970—a rarity in Indian cinema. It failed. Raj Kapoor was emotionally and financially devastated—'*Mera Naam Joker* broke my back, but it built my soul.' But with time, the film came to be recognised as his masterpiece, a cult classic.

As fate willed, he collapsed while being awarded the Dadasaheb Phalke Award for his lifetime contribution. Raj Kapoor taught Indian cinema to dream—with open arms, moist eyes, and an indomitable smile.

PRAKASH MEHRA'S
प्रकाश मेहरा
DUSHMAN

Prakash Mehra

The Man Behind the Angry Young Man

(13 July 1939–17 May 2009)

The year 1973 saw a pivotal film—*Zanjeer*, which pivoted a failed newcomer, Amitabh Bachchan, into superstardom as the 'Angry Young Man', and the filmmaker who had risked casting him when other major stars like Dev Anand and Dharmendra had declined the film was none other than Prakash Mehra.

The '70s had ushered in a new wave of popular cinema—combining action, romance, comedy, and music—known as the 'masala' genre. Mehra's films often centered around the underdog's fight against injustice (*Zanjeer, Laawaris* (1981)), estranged families and lost-and-found themes (*Muqaddar Ka Sikandar* (1987), *Hera Pheri* (2000)), and conflicted heroes torn between duty and love (*Namak Halaal* (1982), *Sharaabi* (1984)).

Grounded in social realities, his movies were crafted with commercial flair, catchy dialogues, and punchy storytelling that resonated across audiences alike. While casting Bachchan in *Zanjeer,* he insisted: 'This man has a volcano inside him. Let him erupt.' People often said Prakash Mehra was to Amitabh what Guru Dutt was to Waheeda Rehman—a director who understood the actor's soul, which Bachchan acknowledged, saying that without *Zanjeer* and Mehra, his career would not have risen the way it did.

However, after a golden run of blockbusters through the '70s and early '80s, the magic began to falter with the failure of *Jaadugar* (1989) due to multiple reasons—the audiences had changed, the genre was different, and with Bachchan facing turbulence in his career, the timing was wrong. Mehra famously trusted his gut more than industry gossip. If he felt a story, a scene, or a song worked emotionally, he would back it completely, even against advice. He worked with a range of big stars across his career—Dharmendra, Vinod Khanna, Anil Kapoor, Rekha, Smita Patil, and Parveen Babi—delivering hit films in numbers. Family and close friends described him as a simple, grounded man, proud of his work but never arrogant. His son Puneet Mehra later tried to carry forward the production banner (Balaji Films), though not with comparable success.

Prakash Mehra left his mark as the quintessential architect of the Bollywood blockbuster—merging the gritty with the glamorous—a blueprint that others would later imitate.

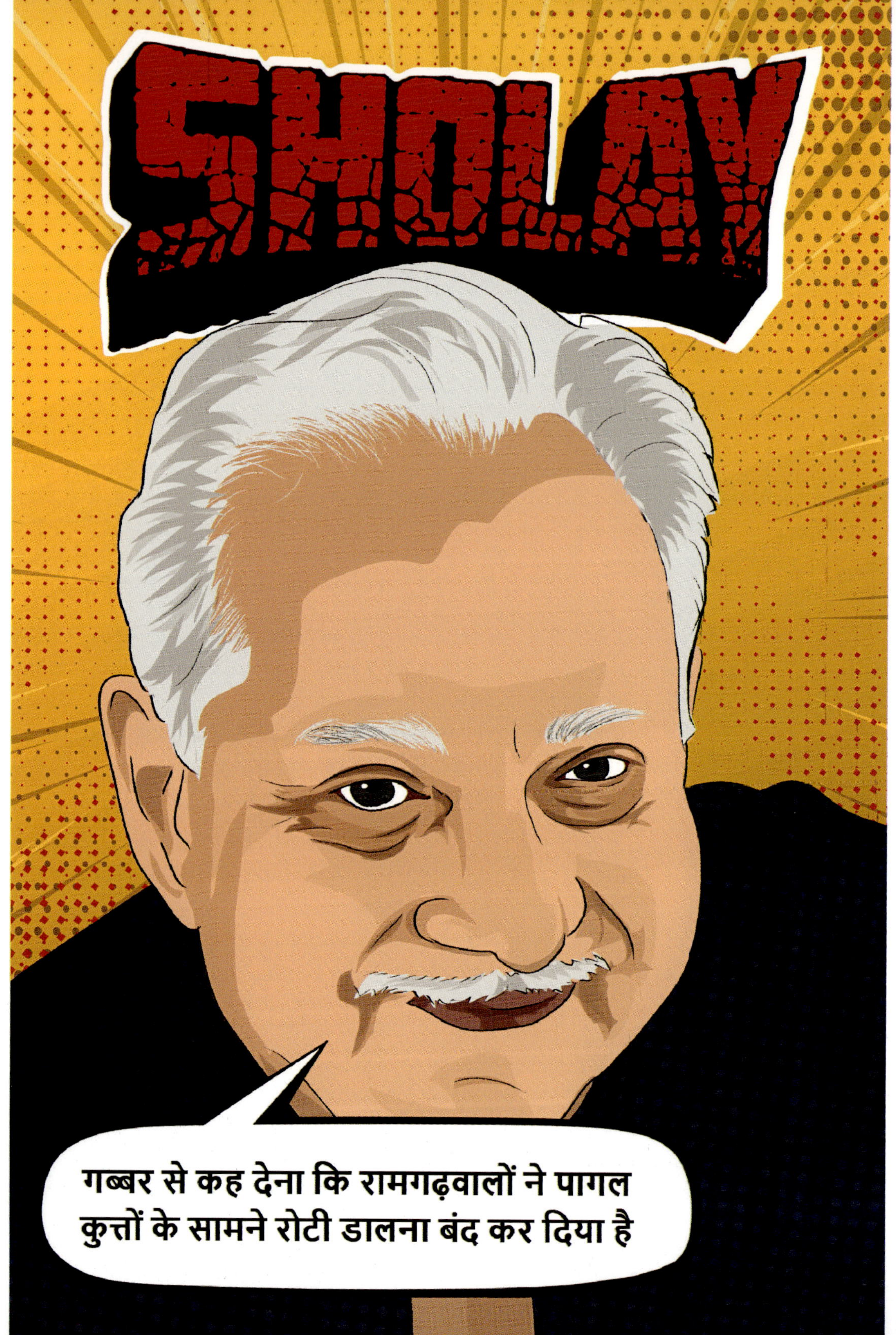
SHOLAY
गब्बर से कह देना कि रामगढ़वालों ने पागल कुत्तों के सामने रोटी डालना बंद कर दिया है

Ramesh Sippy

Blending Stars, Scale, Soul, and Spectacle

(23 January 1947–)

Many directors—Ramesh Sippy, Manmohan Desai, and Yash Chopra—were instrumental in shaping the Bachchan legacy after *Zanjeer*. Ramesh Sippy became a legend after directing *Sholay* (1975), widely considered the most iconic film in Indian cinematic history. Born into a film family—his father, G.P. Sippy, was a famous producer—he entered the industry young and quickly earned a reputation for his large-scale storytelling, technical innovation, and a Hollywood-like visual style. While Prakash Mehra launched Bachchan, Ramesh Sippy and *Sholay* turned him into a cultural phenomenon.

Sippy has innovated technically, too, introducing a new cinematic scale—wide-screen shots, action sequences modeled on Western (cowboy) films, and elaborate character arcs. *Sholay* was one of India's first 70mm widescreen and stereophonic sound films. He has shown mastery over multi-starrer films, perfecting the art of ensemble casting, giving each major character a strong, memorable identity. He has created iconic villains, making Gabbar Singh the most famous villain in Bollywood history.

Unlike directors stuck in one genre, Sippy kept reinventing himself. *Seeta Aur Geeta* (1972), a romantic drama about twin sisters separated at birth, became a template for double-role dramas and made Hema Malini a superstar. *Shaan* (1980) was another grand multi-starrer complete with a flamboyant villain. *Shakti* (1982) was a powerful, emotionally complex father-son drama starring Dilip Kumar and Amitabh Bachchan—two titans of acting. It won critical acclaim, winning the Filmfare Award for Best Film (1983). A love triangle dealing with love, class differences, and emotional longing, *Saagar* (1985) was India's official entry for the Oscars that year and won multiple Filmfare Awards, too.

In 2013, Filmfare honoured Sippy with the Lifetime Achievement Award for his contribution to cinema. After making blockbusters from the '70s to the early '90s, he shifted toward television production (*Buniyaad*, one of India's most iconic TV serials) and mentoring young filmmakers. He launched the Ramesh Sippy Academy of Cinema and Entertainment in Mumbai, nurturing new talent in film and media. Ramesh Sippy, a master craftsman, will be forever remembered for Indian cinema's first truly 'epic' blockbuster.

LIFE IS A ONE-WAY STREET; ONE HAS TO KEEP GOING. FIRST, YOU DEFINE THE WORK FOR YOURSELF AND REMAIN COMMITED TO IT. ONCE THERE IS TOTAL COMMITMENT, THE WORK IN TURN BEGINS TO DEFINE YOU.

Shyam Benegal

The Conscience-Keeper of Indian Cinema

(14 December 1934–23 December 2024)

While 'masala films' captivated masses in the '70s, parallel cinema thrived, with Shyam Benegal and his cinematographer protégé-turned-celebrated director, Govind Nihalani, championing a socially conscious, realist tradition. One of the first Indian filmmakers to centre women's stories without falling into stereotypes, Benegal started his career making advertising films and documentaries, which gave him a strong visual sense and narrative discipline that he carried into his cinema.

Ankur (1974), Benegal's debut, was a quiet yet revolutionary film that exposed caste and gender oppression and launched Shabana Azmi's acting career. *Nishant* (1975) dealt with feudal oppression, while *Bhumika* (1977) was a biography. *Mandi* (1983) took a satirical look at politics and morality through a brothel's micro-society. Benegal mentored a newsreader—Smita Patil—recognising her intense, natural screen presence, and Naseeruddin Shah, who said, 'If not for Shyam Benegal, many of us from NSD (National School of Drama) would have been lost faces in the crowd.' Other great actors who worked with him include Om Puri, Amrish Puri, and Kulbhushan Kharbanda.

Discussions on *Manthan* (1976) focus on how half a million milk producers of rural Gujarat contributed ₹2 each to crowdfund it, making it the first 'people's film'. Based on Verghese Kurien, the father of India's 'White Revolution', and digitally restored and released on the film's fiftieth anniversary at the Cannes Film Festival, Benegal showcased independent India's struggle to engage with modern ideas of economic development and social reform, with powerful Dalit characters as parallel heroes. His later films include a philosophical *Suraj Ka Satvan Ghoda* (1992). He turned to television with a scholarly focus, making *Bharat Ek Khoj* (1988), a monumental series on Nehru's *The Discovery of India*. *Samvidhaan* (2014) followed as a docudrama about the making of the Indian Constitution.

Awarded seven National Film Awards, the Padma Shri (1976), the Padma Bhushan (1991), and the Dadasaheb Phalke Award (2005), Benegal won numerous international festival accolades, including at Berlin, Venice, and Chicago. Benegal refused to commercialise his films, always believing that a film must respect the intelligence of its audience.

হাসি দা

Hrishikesh Mukherjee

The Gentle Chronicler of India's Soul

(30 September 1922–27 August 2006)

The credit for showcasing Bachchan's softer, comedic, and middle-class side in films like *Anand* (1971), *Chupke Chupke* (1975), and *Abhimaan* (1973) belongs to Hrishikesh Mukherjee, one of the most beloved and distinctive directors in Indian cinema.

Hrishida, as he was fondly known, started his career as a film editor and later assistant director to the great Bimal Roy—a master of social realism in cinema. Known for creating heartfelt middle-class dramas that were emotionally rich but never melodramatic, Hrishida blended light humour with serious themes like death, illness, unemployment, love, and morality—ordinary people grappling with ordinary problems, but with warmth, empathy, and dignity. His tight narrative structure made most of his films about tow hours or less, sharply edited and economically told, unlike the norm of about three hours for the masala films. His work is often described as the bridge between art cinema and commercial Bollywood films.

Extremely soft-spoken, humble, and private—far from the flamboyant, larger-than-life image of many Bollywood directors, his personal wit was dry, subtle, and affectionate, never caustic or loud. Approaching his actors like a patient teacher, he allowed them room to explore emotions naturally without imposing grand gestures. Mukherjee was known for his deep moral compass, which was reflected in his films. Despite being a massive success, he remained approachable, informal, and almost shy. Amitabh Bachchan once said, 'Hrishikesh Mukherjee never shouted on a set. He didn't need to.'

Having given career-defining roles to actors like Rajesh Khanna, Amitabh Bachchan, Dharmendra, Jaya Bhaduri (Bachchan), Amol Palekar, and many others, his other iconic films include *Guddi* (1971), *Bawarchi* (1972), *Gol Maal* (1979), and *Satyakam* (1969)—the last being his most serious and one of the finest films on ethical living.

He has been awarded the Dadasaheb Phalke Award in 1999 and the Padma Vibhushan in 2001 besides multiple National Film Awards and Filmfare Awards. Till today, his films are studied in film schools as examples of economical storytelling, character depth, and emotional resonance. Hrishida showed that cinema could be light yet profound, fun yet meaningful, and above all, deeply humane.

हर यार वफादार नहीं होता...

Anurag Kashyap

A Cinematic Punch in the Gut

(10 September 1972–)

If Hrishida found drama in the ordinary, Anurag Kashyap has shattered the ordinary to uncover the raw, the violent, and the political that seeths underneath. Where Hrishida offered the comfort of middle-class warmth, Kashyap delivers a cinematic punch in the gut—jagged, restless, and unfiltered.

Born in Gorakhpur, Kashyap studied zoology in Delhi but found himself drawn to street theatre, poetry, and world cinema. The riot-ravaged, politically turbulent India of the '80s and '90s left an indelible impression on him, and it shows in his films—where the violence isn't always physical, but always systemic. Like many outsiders who move to Mumbai, he entered through the margins—ghostwriting scripts, assisting on projects, and sleeping on borrowed mattresses. His breakthrough came as a writer, co-scripting *Satya* (1998) with Saurabh Shukla for director Ram Gopal Varma, a film that birthed 'Mumbai noir'. But even as that gritty underworld saga made waves, Kashyap's own debut as director, *Paanch* (2003), got stalled by the censors for years.

His first major release, *Black Friday* (2004), based on the 1993 Bombay blasts, was part docudrama, part procedural, and entirely unafraid. It was banned for years, but once released, critics hailed its courage. His next few films—*No Smoking* and *Gulaal* (2007 and 2009)—flopped. Kashyap was bruised, broke, but undeterred. Then came *Dev.D* (2009), his acid-soaked retelling of Devdas—part punk musical, part generational manifesto. It reintroduced heartbreak to a new India. But it was *Gangs of Wasseypur* (2012) that made him a legend. A sprawling, two-part saga of coal mafia politics, vengeance, and masculinity in Bihar, it was operatic, blood-soaked, and oddly hilarious. Martin Scorsese later wrote to Kashyap, praising his work—cinephiles called him India's most 'un-Bollywood' director. As he once said in an interview, 'I don't make films to comfort. I make films to confront.'

Kashyap has received multiple accolades, including a National Film Award for *Gangs of Wasseypur* (Special Jury), and the Ordre des Arts et des Lettres from the French government in 2013 for his contribution to world cinema. In a cinema culture too often afraid to ruffle feathers, Anurag Kashyap ruffled the whole bird.

Haider

Vishal Bhardwaj

The Shakespearewallah

(4 August 1965–)

If Kashyap has cracked open Indian cinema's rough, political underbelly, Vishal Bhardwaj sings its dark secrets in haunting, melodic tunes. Where Kashyap wields anger like a blade, Bhardwaj uses melancholy like a brush—crafting cinema where betrayal, ambition, love, and death moved to the rhythm of poetry and folk songs.

Born in a small town of Uttar Pradesh, Vishal's father was a lyricist and poet, and though Vishal dreamed of becoming a cricketer, destiny had other plans. Music found him early. He joined Hindu College in Delhi, and later entered the music industry, first composing jingles and then scoring films, slowly building a reputation for his melodic instinct.

Gulzar's *Maachis* (1996) established him as a serious composer, and Gulzar nudged him towards filmmaking, recognising a storyteller hidden inside the musician. Bhardwaj's first directorial effort, *Makdee* (2002), was a children's film about superstition and fear.

But it was with *Maqbool* (2003), his adaptation of Shakespeare's *Macbeth* set in the Mumbai underworld, that Bhardwaj truly arrived. With actors like Irrfan Khan, Tabu, and Pankaj Kapur at their peak prowess, Bhardwaj created a gangster-film that felt like a classical tragedy. He returned to Shakespeare again with *Omkara* (2006), based on *Othello*, unfolding amidst the politics of caste and criminality in Uttar Pradesh, and *Haider* (2014), his interpretation of *Hamlet*, set against the backdrop of conflict-ridden Kashmir. Each adaptation was not a translation but a transposition—rooting Shakespeare's moral dilemmas deep into the Indian soil, giving them the weight of history, politics, and personal anguish. His compositions—*Naina Thag Lenge, Namak Ishq Ka,* and *Bismil*—are themselves mini-movies, dripping with metaphor and mood.

Though he has flirted with broader comedies (*Kaminey* (2009), *Matru Ki Bijlee Ka Mandola* (2013)), it is in his darker, brooding narratives that Bhardwaj's full power emerges. Bhardwaj has won seven National Film Awards, including Best Music Direction for *Godmother* (1999) *and Ishqiya* (2010) and Best Screenplay for *Omkara* and *Haider*. In interviews, Vishal often cites the influence of poets, not directors, on his creative thinking. Bhardwaj's cinema isn't just motion—it is heartbreak humming through every frame.

बेशूमार मोहब्बत होगी उस बारिश
की बूँद को इस ज़मीन से,
यूँ ही नहीं कोई मोहब्बत मे इतना
गिर जाता है!

Gulzar

When Pauses Beat Punchlines

(18 August 1934–)

If Vishal Bhardwaj composes cinema with heartbreak and rhythm, Gulzar has given Indian cinema a vocabulary of emotional subtlety. Mentor to Bhardwaj, poet to generations, and director of a very distinct kind, Gulzar's films never shouted. They whisper. They linger. They stay.

Born Sampooran Singh Kalra in Dina (Pakistan), Gulzar's life, like others, was split by Partition. Reaching Mumbai, he began working as a garage mechanic while nurturing a love for words. Writing poetry under the name Gulzar, he caught Bimal Roy's attention, who invited him to write for *Bandini* (1963). That song, *Mora Gora Ang Lai Le,* became a classic and launched a lyricist's career that would eventually include *Tere Bina Zindagi Se, Tujhse Naraz Nahi Zindagi, Tere Liye, Chhaiyya Chhaiyya,* and hundreds more.

Not quite content, Gulzar forayed into direction with *Mere Apne* (1971) and followed it with films like *Parichay* (1972) and *Mausam* (1976), exploring human relationships, casting actors who could underplay—like Sanjeev Kumar, Jaya Bhaduri (Bachchan), and later, Naseeruddin Shah. His scripts avoided big arcs and dramatic resolutions; instead, they offered emotional realisations that dawned, not exploded. *Koshish* (1973) portrayed a deaf-mute couple trying to live with dignity, and *Aandhi* (1975) drew national attention for its subtle parallels with Indira Gandhi. *Ijaazat* (1987) was a chamber piece on lost love and mature regret—quiet, textured, and impossibly modern. In *Maachis* (1996), a young Punjabi boy engages in terrorism to fight a bad situation, only to realise its fickleness.

Gulzar moved away from filmmaking in the '90s, but continued writing lyrics, dialogues, and screenplays. In 2009, he won an Academy Award for Best Original Song for *Jai Ho,* capping a career that included five Indian National Film Awards, 22 Filmfare Awards, and one Grammy, plus the Sahitya Akademi Award for Hindi in 2002, and the Padma Bhushan in 2004. The Dadasaheb Phalke Award came in 2013, and in 2024, Gulzar was awarded the Jnanpith, India's highest literary award. Clad in white kurta-pajamas, often walking alone at dusk, he remains the poet of restraint. 'Silences speak louder than noise,' he once said. And in his films, as in his poems, the silences still echo.

KJo

Karan Johar

Gloss and Glamour, Being and Emptiness

(25 May 1972–)

If Gulzar whispers cinema into being, Karan Johar sings it from rooftops clad in designer labels. Where Gulzar's characters wrestled with quiet regret, Johar's dance through heartbreak under a downpour of chiffon, colour, and confessions. Johar redefined Indian cinema as it entered the new millennium ... oozing gloss.

Born into a film family—his father, Yash Johar, founded Dharma Productions—Karan Johar grew up breathing the rarefied air of Bombay's upper film circles. By his own admission, Johar was a lonely and awkward child, finding solace in stories, style, and sentimentality.

Johar's significant break came as an actor, playing Shah Rukh Khan's nerdy friend in *Dilwale Dulhania Le Jayenge* (1995), where he also assisted director Aditya Chopra. But it was behind the camera that his true talent unfolded. In 1998, Johar directed *Kuch Kuch Hota Hai (KKHH)* (1998), not just a blockbuster but a cultural weather event, capturing a generation's imagination. Suddenly, Bollywood was about friendships, first crushes, heartbreaks, and second chances, wrapped in pop culture and western aesthetics. *Kabhi Khushi Kabhie Gham* (2001) and *Kabhi Alvida Naa Kehna* (2006) expanded the universe, the former an extravagant ode to family and filial bonds, and the latter exploring marital dissatisfaction and emotional betrayal. Dharma Productions and Karan Johar became a tastemaker for Bollywood, launching careers—Alia Bhatt, Varun Dhawan, Sidharth Malhotra—producing a staggering array of films. He crafted his public persona with *Koffee with Karan,* a talk show that pulled Bollywood out of its ivory tower into drawing rooms and gossip columns.

Critics have accused Johar of selling a fantasy too detached from ground realities. But Johar has never pretended otherwise. Honoured with multiple Filmfare Awards, including Best Director for *KKHH* and *My Name Is Khan* (2010), in 2020, he was also awarded the Padma Shri. He once said, 'My films are about people who have everything and yet feel they have nothing. That emptiness is my story.' Where others documented the world as it was, Karan Johar crafted the world as we wished it could be—pain and all, but with a great outfit and a soaring song in the background.

जब वी मेट
JAB WE MET
HIGHWAY
LOVE
AAJ KAL
ANYTHING I WANTED TO DO AND ACHIEVE HAS NOT BEEN INFLUENTIAL IN MY LIFE, BUT MY FAILURES HAVE.

Imtiaz Ali

The Wanderer

(16 June 1971–)

If Karan Johar's cinema is about love dressed in designer couture, Imtiaz Ali's is love with blistered feet, tangled hair, and a map with no destination. Where Johar's lovers have homes to return to, Ali's are always leaving—restless, searching, trying to make sense of who they are by running away from everything they know.

Born in Jamshedpur, Ali spent his early childhood moving through small towns, a journey that left a trace of the wandering romantic in him. He began his career not in cinema, but television, directing series like *Imtihaan* (1995) and *Kurukshetra* (1996) before making the leap.

His first feature, *Socha Na Tha* (2005), hinted at themes that would define his work: love as confusion, travel as therapy, and rebellion as a rite of passage. But it was *Jab We Met* (2007) that brought him national attention. A conventional romantic comedy on the surface, in Geet (Kareena Kapoor) and Aditya (Shahid Kapoor), Ali carved out two people at opposite ends of the emotional spectrum who found themselves by getting lost together.

From there, Ali only dug deeper into the psyche of his characters. *Love Aaj Kal* (2009) challenged linear storytelling, juxtaposing two love stories across time. *Rockstar* (2011) remains his most potent work, where love and art combust inside a self-destructive musician played by Ranbir Kapoor. The film was messy, mystical, and wildly romantic—it gained a cult following.

His later films, *Tamasha* (2015) and *Highway* (2014), continue his exploration of identity, freedom, and trauma. *Highway*, in particular, with Alia Bhatt's startling performance as a kidnapped woman who finds liberation on the road, showcased Ali's ability to merge psychological depth with social metaphor.

Imtiaz Ali hasn't received a National Film Award, but he has won numerous popular awards, including Filmfare Awards for Best Dialogue *(Jab We Met)* and critical acclaim that far outweighs trophies. His influence is unmistakable in the way Hindi cinema treats youth, heartbreak, and selfhood today. In his films, love is always in transit—never quite arriving, but always changing you along the way.

KYA TUM MANTALLY CHALLENGED HO MY BWOY?

Farhan and Zoya Akhtar

When It's All in the DNA

(9 January 1974–) (14 October 1972–)

If Imtiaz Ali has given wanderlust an aching, solitary heart, then Farhan and Zoya Akhtar have taken that spirit, dressed it up in designer sunglasses, loaded it into an SUV, and sent it off on a road trip with friends and complicated feelings riding shotgun. Together, the Akhtar siblings have brought to Indian cinema a voice that is modern, urbane, self-aware—never afraid to be both fun and melancholy at once.

Farhan and Zoya grew up in a household where storytelling was stitched into daily life. Dad Javed Akhtar was one half of the legendary screenwriting duo Salim-Javed, and Mom Honey Irani was an actor and scriptwriter herself. Words, wit, and arguments over movies were the soundtrack of their childhood.

Farhan's directorial debut, *Dil Chahta Hai* (2001), was like a breath of fresh sea air, offering a wry, stylish film rooted in friendship and emotional ambivalence, which not only redefined how Indian youth saw themselves on screen but signalled that Hindi cinema had entered a new, post-liberalisation moment. Zoya took longer to step behind the camera, but when she did, it was with a gaze just as distinct. *Luck By Chance* (2009) was her sharp, bittersweet take on the film industry—its illusions, compromises, and betrayals. She followed it with *Zindagi Na Milegi Dobara* (2011), a film about three friends on a soul-searching road trip across Spain. It became a cultural touchstone for a generation learning to negotiate success, fear, and friendship via an Instagram-worthy adventure.

While Farhan also found success as an actor *(Rock On!* and *Bhaag Milkha Bhaag),* singer, and producer, Zoya deepened her directorial voice with *Dil Dhadakne Do* (2015) and *Gully Boy* (2019), the latter a tour de force exploration of class, art, and rebellion, set in Mumbai's rap underground. It was India's official entry to the Oscars.

Farhan has won multiple Filmfare Awards, including Best Director and Best Actor, and Zoya, too, has won the Filmfare Award for Best Director and received critical acclaim at international festivals. In an industry that often confuses sincerity with spectacle, the Akhtars have proved that you could have both—and that sometimes, the biggest journeys are those happening quietly inside.

TIGER
HAI TU
ROAR
ROAR
ROAR
PEEKE
HAI KYA?
ALL IZZ
WELL!
AYE
CHILLI CHICKEN
TERA HEIGHT
KYA HAI RE

Rajkumar Hirani

Giving Cinema a Jadoo Ki Jhappi

(20 November 1962–)

If Farhan and Zoya Akhtar have given modern India its aspirational voice, Rajkumar Hirani has given it a conscience—not by preaching, but by smiling. His cinema wears its heart on its sleeve.

Born in Nagpur to a middle-class Sindhi family, Hirani grew up in a modest home where his father ran a typewriting institute. He studied editing at the Film and Television Institute of India (FTII) and spent years in advertising before he moved into feature films. The editor's eye never left him—his films remain tightly paced and emotionally charged.

His directorial debut came relatively late in 2003, with *Munna Bhai M.B.B.S.*—the kind of film that comes once in a decade, unexpectedly heartwarming, riotously funny, and sneakily profound. Sanjay Dutt's titular gangster fakes his way into a medical college—and ends up dispensing love and 'jadoo ki jhappis'. Hirani got India laughing while also getting it thinking. He followed it up with *Lage Raho Munna Bhai* (2006), where the same character starts seeing visions of Mahatma Gandhi. The film launched a brief but significant revival of 'Gandhigiri.' Hirani had made morality popular again. Then came *3 Idiots* (2009), a seismic hit that didn't just break box office records but triggered nationwide conversations about education, parental pressure, and the tyranny of rote learning. Starring Aamir Khan as Rancho—a character so idealistic and eccentric that he became aspirational for millions, the film became one of the highest-grossing Bollywood films even in China. Hirani's subsequent films, *PK* (2014) and *Sanju* (2018), starring Aamir Khan and Ranbir Kapoor, respectively, continued his blend of satire and sentiment. *PK* questioned religious orthodoxy through the eyes of an alien, while *Sanju* offered a morally shaded portrait of a controversial star.

Winning 11 Filmfare Awards, including Best Director and Best Screenplay, Hirani's films have received both critical and commercial acclaim, with multiple National Awards recognising their impact. Asked once why his stories always end with such clarity, Hirani replied, 'Because life doesn't. So I want to give people something to carry home—not just a memory, but a feeling.' And that feeling, invariably, is hope.

Devdas
a SANJAY LEELA BHANSALI film
produced by BHARAT SHAH

Sanjay Leela Bhansali

Because the Heart is Grand

(24 February 1963–)

Sanjay Leela Bhansali's films sing, mourn, wail, and dazzle. His stories unfold not in living rooms but in halls of mirrors, under chandeliers, through silhouettes and silences choreographed as meticulously as any dance number.

Born in Mumbai, Bhansali grew up in a Gujarati family where his mother worked to support the household after his father's struggles with alcoholism. He studied at the FTII and began his career assisting Vidhu Vinod Chopra on films like *Parinda* and *1942: A Love Story.*

His directorial debut, *Khamoshi: The Musical* (1996), a tender story about a daughter caught between her deaf-mute parents and her dreams, didn't find commercial success, but revealed Bhansali's emotional and musical sensibility. The film, starring Manisha Koirala and Nana Patekar, remains his most restrained work. Then came *Hum Dil De Chuke Sanam* (1999), where Bhansali found his palette—doomed love, familial duty, resplendent frames, and music as emotional language. The film made a star out of Aishwarya Rai. He followed it with *Devdas* (2002), a fever dream of heartbreak, excess, and operatic beauty. The Shah Rukh Khan-Aishwarya-Madhuri starrer was selected as India's official entry to the Oscars and introduced international audiences to Bhansali's aesthetic. Bhansali's cinema is often accused of being 'too much'—too ornate, too emotional, too theatrical. *Goliyon Ki Raasleela Ram-Leela* (2013), *Bajirao Mastani* (2015), and *Padmaavat* (2018) saw him working at an operatic scale—battles, ballads, betrayals—all sculpted with painterly precision. Through these films, he redefined the mainstream historical epic for Indian audiences, where love and honour were inseparable and tragedy inevitable. In 2022, he returned to Bombay with *Gangubai Kathiawadi*, a biographical drama about a brothel madam-turned-political figure, and Alia Bhatt's performance as Gangubai was widely acclaimed.

Sanjay Leela Bhansali has received seven National Film Awards, including Best Direction and Best Screenplay, and multiple Filmfare Awards across categories. In 2015, he was honoured with the Padma Shri. In his cinema, the heart is always on fire—dancing, weeping, and refusing to look away.

Mani Ratnam

Cinema from the Fault Lines

(2 June 1956–)

Sanjay Leela Bhansali's reds and golds contrast sharply with Mani Ratnam's greys and silences—stories entangled in politics, memory, and moral ambiguity. His cinema simmers—there's no easy catharsis.

Born in Madurai, Ratnam was in a corporate career when the call of cinema grew too loud to ignore. Entering the film industry in the '80s through his first film *Pallavi Anu Pallavi* (1983) in Kannada, he went largely unnoticed. His breakthrough came with *Mouna Ragam* (1986), a film about a young woman trapped between past trauma and a forced marriage. Then came *Nayakan* (1987), loosely based on the life of Mumbai don Varadarajan Mudaliar. With Kamal Haasan delivering a career-defining performance and Ratnam at the height of his directorial control, the film became a landmark in Indian cinema and India's official entry to the Oscars, drawing comparisons with *The Godfather.*

Roja (1992) brought terrorism and nationalism into the mainstream through the story of a wife searching for her kidnapped husband in Kashmir. The film, with A.R. Rahman's stunning debut score, was a massive success and became a turning point in Tamil and Indian cinema. He followed it with *Bombay* (1995), a love story set against the backdrop of the 1992 Bombay riots. In *Dil Se* (1998), love and terrorism once again intersect, this time more abstractly, more poetically. His protagonists are often flawed—idealists, journalists, artists, militants—all trying to live honestly in a world that rarely allows it. In later films, like *Kannathil Muthamittal, Guru, Raavanan,* and *Ponniyin Selvan*, Ratnam continued to expand his canvas—experimenting with folklore, history, and corporate ambition.

Mani Ratnam has received six National Film Awards, several Filmfare Awards South, and in 2002, he was honoured with the Padma Shri. He is widely credited with redefining Tamil and Indian cinema's visual language. In interviews, he rarely elaborates, preferring his films to do the speaking. Mani Ratnam's cinema lives in the fault lines—lyrical, unsettling, and profoundly human.

YEARS
DIRECTED BY VETRIMAARA
MUSIC BY G. V. PRAKASH KU
ANANDHI | AADUKALAM MURUGADOS
Paava
Kadhaig

Vetrimaaran

Because Once You Look, You Cannot Unsee

(4 September 1975–)

If Mani Ratnam lights a political fire beneath love stories, then Vetrimaaran steps directly into the fire and films what he finds there—corruption, caste, injustice, brutality, and the slow-burning resilience of people denied dignity. There is nothing ornamental about his cinema. It does not romanticise revolution. It documents it—sometimes with anger, sometimes grief.

Born in Cuddalore, Tamil Nadu, Vetrimaaran studied literature in Chennai. After assisting director Balu Mahendra, Vetrimaaran made his debut with *Polladhavan* (2007), a film about a man whose stolen bike becomes the catalyst for a confrontation with crime and power. The premise was minor, but the treatment was bold, psychological, and unusually grounded for commercial Tamil cinema then.

His next film, *Aadukalam* (2011), exploded all expectations. Starring Dhanush as a cockfighting champion caught in a web of ego and betrayal, it became a critical and commercial success, winning six National Film Awards, including Best Director and Best Actor. It signaled the arrival of a director who could fuse craft with conscience, folklore with structural commentary. With *Visaranai* (2015), he turned his gaze to the underbelly of the justice system. Based on a real-life account of a Tamil auto-driver, it is not an easy film to watch—but an essential one. *Visaranai* was India's official entry to the Academy Awards that year and brought Vetrimaaran international recognition for his raw, documentary-like style and moral ferocity. In *Vada Chennai* (2018), he returned to the gangster genre, but turned it inside out—placing his protagonist at the heart of a political conspiracy that spans decades, neighbourhoods, and prison cells. His follow-up, *Asuran* (2019), was a searing caste-revenge drama, also starring Dhanush, which won the National Film Award for Best Feature Film in Tamil.

Vetrimaaran has become one of India's most vital cinematic voices and continues to push Tamil cinema into urgent political terrain—without compromise. When asked why he chooses such harsh, unrelenting subjects, he said, 'These are not stories from the margins. They are the majority. We've just been trained not to look at them.' Vetrimaaran insists that we look—and once you do, his cinema doesn't allow you to unsee.

உலகம்

Kamal Haasan

Because the Questions Never Cease

(7 November 1954–)

Kamal Haasan has taught the audience that cinema can be anything—political essay, psychological thriller, mythic opera, or silent scream—and still move you, entertain you, and challenge your intellect. There has perhaps never been a more shape-shifting figure in Indian cinema. As actor, writer, director, producer, lyricist, dancer, and now politician, Kamal Haasan is less a man and more an institution constantly reinventing itself.

Born in Paramakudi, Tamil Nadu, to a lawyer father and a devout mother, Kamal Haasan was a child prodigy. He entered the film industry at the age of six, winning the President's Gold Medal for his performance in *Kalathur Kannamma* (1960). What followed was a career that has spanned over six decades, hundreds of films, and several languages—a sheer range of roles, the fearlessness with which he tackled taboo subjects, and the belief that cinema could be both artistic and deeply political.

Haasan's directorial debut, *Hey Ram* (2000), was a shock to the system. A bilingual historical thriller about Partition, nationalism, and the assassination of Mahatma Gandhi, the film was dense, provocative, and formally audacious. He followed it with *Virumaandi* (2004), a Rashomon-style prison drama that explored capital punishment, rural feuds, and the slipperiness of truth. In *Dasavathaaram* (2008), his flamboyant outing, he acted and played ten different roles across centuries in a story that was part sci-fi, part religious satire, part metaphysical puzzle.

Kamal Haasan's films, always ahead of their time, have faced delays, censorship issues, or box office struggles upon release, only to be celebrated years later as visionary. His passion for technology, prosthetics, stunts, and narrative experimentation has inspired a generation of Tamil filmmakers to think beyond formula.

Haasan has been honoured with four National Film Awards, the Padma Shri (1990), and the Padma Bhushan (2014). His contributions as a filmmaker have been recognised not just in India but across international circuits. In his films, questions about justice, violence, identity, and freedom echo long after the credits roll.

இயக்குநர்
சிகரம்

K. Balachander

What If?

(9 July 1930–23 December 2014)

Kamal Haasan has often credited Balachander as his guru. It was Balachander who gave him early roles in *Arangetram (1973)*, *Apoorva Raagangal* (1975), and later *Ek Duuje Ke Liye* (1981). In the southern film industry, Balachander was not merely a director—he was a discoverer who found talent, forged it, and often bent the narrative to spotlight characters, conflicts, and conversations that were long kept out of the frame.

Kailasam Balachander came from a middle-class family and began his career not in cinema but in theatre and later, in the civil service. But writing remained his true calling. By the early '60s, he was writing plays that questioned patriarchy, bureaucracy, and the hypocrisies of social norms with sharp wit and emotional force. That clarity of voice found its way into his films, which were unlike anything else Tamil cinema had seen then.

His directorial breakthrough came with *Neerkumizhi* (1965), adapted from one of his own stage plays. From there, Balachander built a body of work that examined women's agency, caste rigidity, marital strain, and institutional cruelty, all within the accessible grammar of mainstream cinema. In *Arangetram,* he told the story of a Brahmin girl who becomes a sex worker to support her large orthodox family. In *Aval Oru Thodar Kathai* (1974), he followed a young working woman burdened with endless familial obligations. These were not just bold films; they were socially disruptive. But Balachander's influence extends far beyond Kamal Haasan. He launched or mentored actors like Rajinikanth, Sridevi, Saritha, Sujatha, and even directors like Vasanth and Suresh Krissna. His production house, Kavithalayaa Productions, became a hub for intelligent, emotionally rich storytelling in Tamil cinema throughout the '80s and '90s.

Balachander was honoured with the Padma Shri (1987), the Dadasaheb Phalke Award (2010), and multiple National Film Awards and Filmfare Awards South. But his true legacy lies in the actors he launched, the taboos he dismantled, and the scripts that whispered radicalism in simple lines. His stories are not revolutionary. But they ask, 'what if?' And in that 'what if', Balachander quietly remade the moral architecture of popular Indian cinema.

YOU CANNOT ENGRAVE ON WATER, NOR WOUND IT WITH A KNIFE, WHICH IS WHY THE RIVER HAS NO FEAR OF MEMORIES

Girish Karnad

The Art of Confrontation

(19 May 1938–10 June 2019)

If Balachander drew cinematic drama from everyday hypocrisies, Girish Karnad reached further back—into mythology, folklore, and history—to illuminate the deep structures of Indian identity. Where Balachander wrote for the street, Karnad wrote for the stage, but when he turned to cinema, his vision was just as potent. He wasn't a prolific filmmaker, but what he made asked enduring, uneasy questions about power, gender, culture, and what it meant to be civilised.

Born in Matheran, then part of the Bombay Presidency, Karnad was raised in Karnataka and educated in Dharwad. A Rhodes Scholar at Oxford, he could have chosen any number of elite paths—academia, diplomacy, administration—but Karnad was drawn to stories—first to plays, then to films. His early plays in Kannada theatre—*Yayati, Tughlaq,* and *Hayavadana*—reinterpreted classical and mythological sources through modern, often existential lenses. He was fluent in multiple languages, but Kannada became his literary and cinematic anchor. Karnad debuted as a screenwriter and actor in *Samskara* (1970), directed by P. Rama Reddy, widely considered the starting point of the parallel cinema in Karnataka. Karnad's face became one of the defining images of art-house cinema: sharp-eyed, introspective, and burning with repressed conflict. His directorial debut, *Vamsha Vriksha* (1971), co-directed with B.V. Karanth, focused on widow remarriage, generational trauma, and social reform. His 1973 film *Kaadu* looked at tribal and forest life, and *Ondanondu Kaladalli* (1978), a medieval action drama with samurai-film undertones, is remembered for its formal beauty and sparse, poetic storytelling. Karnad's cinema was deeply rooted in Indian traditions but never nostalgic. He acted in and directed films across languages—Hindi, Kannada, Marathi, Malayalam—becoming a rare public intellectual who straddled the literary, cinematic, and political worlds with equal fluency.

Awarded the Padma Shri in 1974, Padma Bhushan in 1992, the Jnanpith Award in 1998, and multiple National Film Awards both as actor and filmmaker, Karnad saw himself more as a writer or a director. He always forced India to confront itself.

পুলু

Basu Chatterjee

The Middle Cinema Man

(10 January 1927–4 June 2020)

Basu Chatterjee entered cinema through the documentary division of Films Division and then worked under Basu Bhattacharya and Hrishikesh Mukherjee before making his directorial debut with *Sara Akash* in 1969—a film that quietly announced the arrival of a new kind of realism.

This realism—fondly remembered as the 'middle cinema' of the '70s and '80s—positioned itself between the melodrama of commercial Bollywood and the abstraction of parallel cinema. Alongside Hrishida, Chatterjee made films that felt lived-in, modest in scale but vast in empathy. His characters weren't heroes or revolutionaries—they were clerks, typists, bachelors, housewives, all navigating love, disappointment, and routine with understated courage. His films chuckled, sighed, and occasionally sang along to the radio.

Born in Ajmer, Chatterjee began as an illustrator and cartoonist for *Blitz*, the tabloid. It's no surprise that his visual style was economical, observant, and sharply human. In *Rajnigandha* (1974), a working woman must choose between a dependable lover and a charismatic ex, where no one is villainous—just human. *Chhoti Si Baat* (1976) remains one of Hindi cinema's gentlest comedies. *Baton Baton Mein* (1979) is practically a hymn to the Mumbai local train—a love story that unfolds between Churchgate and Borivali. With *Piya Ka Ghar* (1971), *Khatta Meetha* (1979), and *Shaukeen* (1982), he turned domestic life into delightful theatre, treating everyday problems as rich narrative material. Chatterjee was also prolific in television, directing *Byomkesh Bakshi,* arguably the most beloved detective series in Indian broadcasting history. His films, often scored with easy-going Kishore Kumar melodies and populated by talents like Amol Palekar, Vidya Sinha, and Ashok Kumar, offered comfort without ever being sentimental.

Basu Chatterjee received a Filmfare Award and was honoured with the IIFA Lifetime Achievement Award. In 2020, the IIFA Awards recognised his legacy with a special honour. Though not as decorated as his contemporaries, his influence is unmistakable in today's urban, character-driven indie films. In film after film, Chatterjee understood India's middle class long before anyone else thought it was worth writing about.

DO BIGHA ZAMIN
BIMAL ROY
Bimal Roy PRODUCTIONS
THE SILENT
MASTER

Bimal Roy

Chronicler of the Quiet Sorrows

(12 July 1909–7 January 1966)

Bimal Roy's tender, tragic cinema was the soil from which directors like Basu Chatterjee and Hrishikesh Mukherjee later grew. He gave cinematic voice to quiet sorrows—the kind borne by farmers, widows, labourers, and outcasts. His cinema was unafraid of melancholy, but never hopeless; it dignified suffering without romanticising it. In a decade when Hindi cinema was veering toward melodrama and musical flourish, Roy insisted on restraint, subtlety, and moral clarity.

Roy came of age in the politically charged air of pre-Independence India. He began his film career at New Theatres in Calcutta, working under the legendary Nitin Bose as a cinematographer and editor, before making his directorial debut in the late '40s. With the Partition looming, Roy moved to Bombay, carrying with him the literary and artistic sensibilities of the Bengal Renaissance.

It was with *Do Bigha Zamin* (1953) that Roy's voice found its full expression. The story of a poor farmer who travels to Calcutta to earn money and save his land from an oppressive zamindar, the film was stark, realist, and devastatingly tender. It established Roy as a filmmaker of conscience. His subsequent work deepened that legacy. *Parineeta* (1953), *Biraj Bahu* (1954), and *Devdas* (1955) all took literary source materials and infused them with deep human feelings and formal elegance. In *Madhumati* (1958), Roy dabbled in reincarnation and gothic mystery, but still grounded the narrative in longing and loss. He also directed *Sujata* (1959), a poignant story about caste discrimination and adoption, and *Bandini* (1963), one of his most emotionally layered films, about a woman prisoner grappling with love, betrayal, and guilt. *Bandini* was Nutan's triumph, but it was Roy's quiet direction that made it unforgettable.

Roy received 11 Filmfare Awards, including Best Director and Best Film, a National Film Award, and international recognition at Cannes. He was posthumously honoured with the Padma Shri in 1962. In a time of grand gestures and heightened theatrics, Bimal Roy held up a mirror—cracked by hardship, clouded by injustice, but still capable of reflecting grace.

THE DREAMERS CHANGE BUT THE DREAMS REMAIN THE SAME.

Mahesh Bhatt

The Aching Mess of Being Human

(20 September 1948–)

Mahesh Bhatt puts sorrow on the screen raw, bleeding, and barely clothed. His cinema isn't about aesthetic tragedy—it is about inner collapse and personal betrayal. Few directors have exposed themselves as nakedly as Bhatt has in his most formative films.

Bhatt comes from a complicated family—a Hindu Brahmin filmmaker father, Nanabhai Bhatt, and a Muslim mother, Shirin Mohammad Ali, whom he never saw as part of a conventional marriage. The duality, secrecy, and fracture in his early domestic life formed the emotional grammar of his later works. Raised without his father's name on school forms, Bhatt grew up on the margins of legitimacy—wrestling with identity, shame, and longing.

Beginning his career in the '70s with *Manzilein Aur Bhi Hain* (1974), which ran into trouble with the censors for its themes of crime and morality, it was with *Arth* (1982) that he truly arrived. Drawn from his real-life extramarital affair with actress Parveen Babi, it was a breakthrough in how Hindi cinema depicted marriage, betrayal, and a woman's emotional awakening. Shabana Azmi's performance as a wife who chooses dignity over dependence remains one of the most powerful feminist arcs in Indian cinema. He followed it with *Saaransh* (1984), a heartbreaking study of old age, loss, and bureaucratic apathy, and then *Janam* (1985) and *Naam* (1986), both laced with themes of illegitimacy, identity, and fractured parenthood. In *Daddy* (1989), he gave Pooja Bhatt, his daughter, her debut in a role that mirrored her own father's demons—alcoholism, redemption, and fragile love.

In the '90s, Bhatt pivoted to making formulaic, but always watchable films. He launched talents like Anu Agarwal *(Aashiqui (1990))*, Rahul Roy, and Sonu Nigam, and under the Vishesh Films banner with brother Mukesh Bhatt, he delivered major hits—*Raaz* (2002), *Murder* (2004), *Zeher* (2005), *Jannat* (2008)—that redefined the musical-thriller template. Mahesh Bhatt was awarded the National Film Award for *Saaransh,* while *Arth* and *Daddy* remain critical benchmarks in psychological realism. Asked why his films are so deeply personal, he said, 'Cinema is not about perfect people. It's about wounded people finding the courage to live.' For a brief, searing period in Indian cinema, Mahesh Bhatt showed those wounds without makeup.

MOGAMBO... KHUSH HUA!
MAI HU
PHOOLAN DEVI!

Shekhar Kapur

The Truth Inside the Myth

(6 December 1945–)

Shekhar Kapur's cinema asks not only who we are, but how the forces of history, myth, and conquest shape that question. He is a director of global vision and personal restlessness—forever chasing the ineffable through both intimate drama and grand spectacle.

Born in Lahore before Partition, Kapur came from a family of lawyers and film personalities. His mother was the sister of legendary actor Dev Anand. Shekhar studied economics in London and became a chartered accountant before restlessness—his lifelong fuel—drew him to the camera.

He began as an actor, but his true calling emerged behind the lens. His directorial debut, *Masoom* (1983), a delicate chamber piece about a family torn apart by the arrival of an illegitimate child, showcased Kapur's gift for emotional texture. Anchored by performances from Naseeruddin Shah and Shabana Azmi, it remains one of the most affecting domestic dramas in Indian cinema. *Mr. India* (1987) made him a household name. A superhero film before the genre existed in India, it combined humour, fantasy, satire, and unforgettable characters—especially Amrish Puri's villainous Mogambo. True to form, Kapur didn't stay long in that genre either. In the '90s, setting his sights westward, he made *Bandit Queen* (1994), a brutally honest biopic of Phoolan Devi. Shot in raw landscapes with an almost documentary intensity, the film is a harrowing account of caste, gender violence, and vengeance. It faced censorship, but won international acclaim, announcing Kapur as a force in global independent cinema. And then came *Elizabeth* (1998). With Cate Blanchett's career-making performance and Kapur's painterly eye, this English-language period drama about the early reign of Queen Elizabeth I became a critical and commercial success. It was nominated for seven Academy Awards. He followed it with *Elizabeth: The Golden Age* (2007).

Shekhar Kapur received the Padma Shri in 2000 and the British Academy of Film and Television Arts (BAFTA) Award for Best British Film for *Elizabeth.* He has served on international film juries at Cannes and Venice—an influential voice in cross-cultural filmmaking. His cinema chases the emotional truth inside the myth.

IF WE DON'T TELL OUR OWN STORIES, NO ONE ELSE WILL.

Mira Nair

Rooted in India

(15 October 1957–)

If Kapur's cinema traverses palaces and power, Mira Nair's sets foot in the everyday—markets, courtyards, university halls, and bustling immigrant enclaves. Her stories explore identity, exile, and the burden of history—one of the first Indian-born filmmakers to make a global name not by escaping her roots, but by examining them with unflinching tenderness and truth.

Born in a middle-class Punjabi family, Mira left for Harvard at 19 to study acting but turned to documentary filmmaking. Her early short works, such as *So Far from India* (1983), chronicled an Indian migrant's double life between Gujarat and New York.

Her first narrative feature, *Salaam Bombay!* (1988), exploded onto the world stage. Made with street children, on location, and largely without stars, the film was a searing portrait of life on Mumbai's margins. It won the Camera d'Or at Cannes and was nominated for an Academy Award. She followed this with *Mississippi Masala* (1991), starring Denzel Washington and Sarita Choudhury, which explored love across race, class, and the legacy of the Ugandan Asian expulsion. From then on, Nair carved out her space—films at the intersection of diaspora and homeland, the personal and the political, making *The Perez Family* (1995), *The Namesake* (2006), and *Queen of Katwe* (2016). *Monsoon Wedding* (2001) remains her most celebrated film. A whirlwind of song, colour, secrets, and family politics, set during a Punjabi wedding in Delhi, it won the Golden Lion at the Venice Film Festival—making Nair the first Indian woman to do so—and was later adapted into a stage musical. Nair also founded the Maisha Film Lab, a non-profit dedicated to nurturing young filmmakers in Uganda and the wider region.

Mira received the Padma Bhushan in 2021, alongside a BAFTA nomination, multiple Independent Spirit Awards, and global festival honours. Her films have premiered at Venice, Cannes, Berlin, and Toronto, and she remains one of the most influential women directors from the Global South.

She once said, 'I am at home in the world. But I carry India inside me.' In film after film, she opens that world up—showing how far India travels, and how deeply it stays.

Heaven on Earth
A film by Deepa Mehta
EARTH
DEEPA MEHTA

Deepa Mehta

Breaking the Taboos

(15 September 1950–)

Mira Nair has carried India across borders with warmth and wit. Deepa Mehta has set fire to its unspoken traumas—literally. Her films are confrontational, poetic, and political. Few directors, especially women, have endured the backlash she has for asking—what happens when society refuses to reckon with its injustices?

Raised in a Punjabi household in Amritsar, with a mother who loved movies and a father who distributed them, Deepa married Canadian filmmaker Paul Saltzman and moved to Toronto in the '70s. Here, she began crafting films on the fraught intersection between India's inherited traditions and the modern individual's right to question them. With modest early films like *Sam & Me* (1991), it was the *Elements Trilogy—Fire* (1996), *Earth* (1998), and *Water* (2005)—that catapulted her into fame and controversy. *Fire* tells the story of two neglected sisters-in-law who find love and intimacy in each other. Among the first mainstream Indian films to depict a lesbian relationship, it became a flashpoint in the culture wars of the late '90s, getting pulled off from cinemas. Mehta received death threats. But the film endured, becoming a rallying point for conversations on sexual freedom, women's rights, and artistic censorship. *Earth* dealt with the Partition through the eyes of a young girl in Lahore, bearing witness to the communal bloodbath around her. Featuring powerful performances from Aamir Khan and Nandita Das, nominated for Best Foreign Film at the Oscars, it is one of the most harrowing cinematic depictions of Partition.

But it was *Water* that proved most controversial. Shot initially in Varanasi, the film explored the lives of widows banished to ashrams in colonial India. Production had to be shut down in 2000 after violent protests, and it took five years before Mehta completed the film in Sri Lanka. Released in 2005, it was met with international acclaim and earned an Academy Award nomination.

Deepa Mehta has received the Order of Canada, their highest civilian honour, and numerous international awards, including at Berlin, Toronto, and San Sebastián. With her trilogy, she forced a nation to remember what it would rather forget.

কত সুখ দুখ কত
মুখ
যে

Rituparno Ghosh

The Fluidity of Being

(31 August 1963–30 May 2013)

Rituparno Ghosh's cinema disarms with its vulnerability—it's not a battle cry, but a series of whispered truths—about longing, loneliness, fluidity, and the unbearable tenderness of being. Where others staged gender and identity as subjects, Ghosh lived them. His films are like private letters—lush, introspective, theatrical, and brave.

Born into a Bengali middle-class family steeped in art and literature, Ghosh was influenced by Tagore's literary modernism and Ray's visual poise—his aesthetics unmistakably Bengali—elegant interiors, silences that spoke, and characters weighing emotion against duty.

His debut feature *Hirer Angti* (1994), a children's film, gave little hint of what was to come. It was *Unishe April* (1994) that announced his arrival. Starring Aparna Sen and Debashree Roy, the film examined the strained relationship between a mother and daughter, both performing women in their own right—one on stage, the other in life. It won the National Award for Best Feature Film. With films like *Dahan* (1997), *Bariwali* (1999), and *Utsab* (2000), Ghosh charted the internal landscapes of women in urban and semi-urban Bengal—mothers, wives, daughters, widows—all caught between tradition and self-expression. His camera lingered on faces, spaces, and objects longer than necessary, drawing the audience into an emotional claustrophobia but never as a voyeur.

Ghosh was among the first Indian filmmakers to bring gender non-conformity into the mainstream. As his gender identity evolved—from a gay man to someone embracing a more fluid, feminine expression—so did his work. *Chitrangada* (2012) mirrored his personal exploration of identity. Even earlier, in *Arekti Premer Golpo* (2010), where he played a documentary filmmaker investigating queer love, the lines between autobiography and fiction blurred with rare honesty. He also wrote columns, hosted television shows, and acted, becoming an icon for the LGBTQ+ community in India. Winning 12 National Film Awards and multiple international recognitions, Ghosh left behind a body of work that expanded the emotional vocabulary of Indian cinema. Asked whether he made 'women's films' he replied, 'I make films about people who feel deeply. If that makes them women's films, so be it.' In his deeply felt, deeply lived cinema, everyone had permission to feel.

Saari Raat
ALL REGIONS

Aparna Sen

Truth Just Happens to Come from a Woman

(25 October 1945–)

If Ghosh gave Bengali cinema its softest voice of defiance, Aparna Sen has given it its most articulate one. Hers is a cinema of precision, poise, and a quiet insistence on nuance. She, too, explores the emotional interiors of women's lives. But while Ghosh's lens often lingered like a lover's, hers observes like a diarist: exact, sensitive, and deeply literary.

Sen's father was Chidananda Dasgupta, a pioneering film critic, documentary filmmaker, and a founder of the Calcutta Film Society along with Satyajit Ray. It was Ray who gave her her first acting role in *Teen Kanya* (1961) at age 16. While she became one of Bengali cinema's most beloved actors, it was behind the camera that she found her fullest expression.

Sen's directorial debut, *36 Chowringhee Lane* (1981), is a quiet marvel. The story of an ageing Anglo-Indian schoolteacher living alone in post-Independence Calcutta, the film is a meditation on loneliness, obsolescence, and memory. It won the National Film Award for Best Direction.

Over the years, Sen often returned to women at crossroads—caught between tradition and autonomy, motherhood and selfhood. In *Paroma* (1984), a housewife's extramarital affair with a photographer unravels not only her marriage but her very sense of self. *Sati* (1989) dealt with superstition and widowhood in nineteenth-century Bengal, while *Yugant* (1995) quietly embedded environmental anxiety in a crumbling marriage.

With *Mr. and Mrs. Iyer* (2002), a tale of communal tension disguised as a travelog—it follows a Tamil Brahmin woman and a Muslim photographer (played by her daughter Konkona Sen Sharma and Rahul Bose, respectively) as they navigate a terror attack during a bus journey—was both a tender love story and a piercing critique of bigotry.

Sen has won three National Film Awards, several Bengal Films Journalists' Association (BFJA) Awards, and the Padma Shri (1987). Her cinema continues to evolve, most recently with *The Rapist* (2021), a raw exploration of trauma and justice. In her films lie the power of her voice, always watching the world from a corner seat with a notepad in hand.

വണ്ടർ
എന്നീ

Anjali Menon

Rhythms from the Backwaters

(20 December 1979–)

From the sunlit verandahs and bustling kitchens of contemporary Kerala, Anjali Menon's cinema enters like an old friend, arms full of memories, laughter, grief, and food. And in that deceptively gentle arrival lies its quiet revolution.

Born in Kozhikode and raised partly in Dubai, Anjali Menon grew up straddling multiple cultures. She studied communication and film in Pune and London before returning to Kerala—not just to make films, but to listen to its changing rhythms and translate them to the screen with empathy and freshness.

Her debut feature, *Manjadikuru* (2008), was a coming-of-age tale told through the eyes of a ten-year-old boy visiting his ancestral home after his grandfather's death. It wasn't just a story about childhood; it was about the passage of time, the erosion of feudal structures, and the unspoken fractures within families. Though the film took years to find its theatrical release, it earned critical acclaim and won several awards, including the Fédération Internationale de la Presse Cinématographique (FIPRESCI) Prize and the Best Film, Best Director, Best Screenplay, Best Cinematography, and Best Upcoming Talent prizes at the South Asian International Film Festival. But it was *Bangalore Days* (2014) that made her a household name. Written and directed by Menon, the film followed three cousins navigating young adulthood in the titular city. On the surface, it was light and breezy—a celebration of youth, friendship, and second chances. But under the charm lay deeply modern concerns: disability and romance, gender roles, the tyranny of career expectations, and the immigrant experience.

In *Koode* (2018), Menon returned to a more sombre terrain—loss, trauma, and healing within a broken family, featuring some of the most nuanced portrayals of mental health in recent Malayalam cinema. She has won several Kerala State Film Awards, Filmfare Awards South, and was awarded Best Director at the Indian Film Festival of Los Angeles. She has also been a vocal advocate for better gender representation in Indian cinema, co-founding the Women in Cinema Collective (WCC) in Kerala—a platform that emerged in response to systemic gender-based injustices in the industry. Anjali Menon continues to build a cinema of care—unassuming, inclusive, and always deeply humane.

CINEMA CAN'T BE A CASUAL AFFAIR...IT HAS TO BE A SINGLE-MINDED PASSION

Adoor Gopalakrishnan

Because Silence Speaks Louder

(3 July 1941–)

If Anjali Menon has given modern Kerala cinema its softest embrace, Adoor Gopalakrishnan has given it its most rigorous gaze, unfolding in silence—long, contemplative silences where time slows and thought deepens. His cinema meditates, doesn't seek applause—it demands engagement. Born in Travancore, Adoor was among the first graduates of the FTII in Pune, where he studied direction in the early 1960s. This generation would become synonymous with India's parallel cinema movement.

His debut feature *Swayamvaram* (1972)—a stark, layered portrait of a couple who defy tradition only to find themselves crushed by economic and social disillusionment—became the first Malayalam film to receive the National Film Award for Best Film. The dialogues are is few, the performances subdued, and yet the tension is palpable. Adoor went on to direct just over a dozen feature films in a career spanning five decades, each one a masterclass in restraint and philosophical inquiry. *Kodiyettam* (1977) followed a man-child's slow awakening to adulthood and responsibility, a metaphor for India's own coming of age. *Mukhamukham* (1984) explored disillusionment with political idealism through the story of a vanished revolutionary. *Mathilukal* (1990) was a tender and lyrical tale of love between two inmates who never see each other, communicating only through a wall. His films have little in the way of a conventional plot. They are more concerned with moral weather—the silent churn of conscience, the long arc of change, and the poetic stillness of rural life. Adoor's collaborations with cinematographer Mankada Ravi Varma and actors like Bharat Gopy helped establish a distinct visual and performative style—unhurried, spare, and profoundly humane.

Adoor Gopalakrishnan has received 16 National Film Awards, including Best Director multiple times, and 35 Kerala State Film Awards. He was awarded the Padma Shri (1984), the Dadasaheb Phalke Award (2004), and the Padma Vibhushan (2006). His films have premiered and been honoured at festivals like Venice, Cannes, Berlin, and Toronto. Most truths happen in slience, and in that slience, Adoor's films continue to speak in ways that echo long after the final frame.

PIONEER OF PARALLEL
CINEMA

Girish Kasaravalli

Immersed in the Stillness

(3 December 1950–)

If Adoor has forged the meditative core of Malayalam cinema, Girish Kasaravalli has carved out its Kannada counterpart—no less philosophical, no less rigorous, and equally rooted in local soil. While Adoor explored silence, Kasaravalli often explored stillness—his camera lingering on the passing of time, the erosion of tradition, and the negotiation between individual agency and collective history.

Like Adoor, Kasaravalli landed at FTII, where he was a contemporary of filmmakers like Saeed Akhtar Mirza and Ketan Mehta. But unlike many peers who moved toward Hindi or crossover cinema, Kasaravalli stayed close to Kannada, its rhythms, and its regional truths. His debut feature *Ghatashraddha* (1977) was a quiet storm. Set in an orthodox Brahmin household, it's the story of a young widow who becomes pregnant and is subjected to ritual ostracisation. Austere in its visuals and devastating in its emotional impact, the film won the National Award for Best Feature Film and is still hailed as a landmark.

Over the years, Kasaravalli's work was marked by intellectual precision and emotional subtlety. *Tabarana Kathe* (1987), about a retired government servant's Kafkaesque struggle to receive his pension, and *Thaayi Saheba* (1997), about a woman navigating power, love, and political change during the pre-Independence era, both won National Awards for Best Feature Film. His films consistently returned to themes of gender, caste, rural transformation, and the loneliness of moral clarity in a corrupt world. He often adapted literary works to explore their deeper philosophical concerns. Even in later films like *Dweepa* (2002), which tackled displacement due to dam projects, or *Kanasemba Kudureyaneri* (2010), about a dreamer caught between superstition and prophecy, Kasaravalli preserved his signature austerity while engaging with urgent socio-political themes.

Having won four National Film Awards for Best Feature Film, the most by any Indian filmmaker in that category, he has also received the Padma Shri (2011), numerous Karnataka State Film Awards, and international festival honours in Rotterdam, Cairo, and Tokyo. Believing that cinema is not for slogans but for questions, through every quiet frame, Kasaravalli asks the kind of questions that echo, not just in the mind, but in the conscience.

IT'S DIFFICULT TO BECOME THE RICHEST MAN ON EARTH, BUT IT'S MORE DIFFICULT TO BE AND REMAIN A GOOD HUMAN BEING.

Jahnu Barua

Landscapes of Assamese Life

(18 October 1952–)

Jahnu Barua tunes his cinema to the quiet cadences of Assam. Where many regional filmmakers battle for visibility, Barua makes films so rooted, so humane, and so resonant that they rise above boundaries. He has become not only Assam's most celebrated filmmaker but one of Indian cinema's most tender chroniclers of resilience.

Born in Sivasagar, he studied physics before shifting to FTII, where he trained in direction. His debut feature, *Aparoopa* (1982), was an intimate, quietly devastating look at a woman's life within the constraints of an unequal marriage and a stifling society. But it was with *Halodhia Choraye Baodhan Khai* (1987)—*The Catastrophe*, as translated internationally—that Barua reached his artistic zenith. The film, about an old farmer dispossessed of his land by powerful interests, unfolds with a grace that belies its political fury.

Halodhia Choraye... won the National Award for Best Feature Film, the Golden Lotus, and brought Assamese cinema into international focus by winning the World Peace Prize at the Chicago International Film Festival. Barua's later films, including *Firingoti* (1992), *Xagoroloi Bohudoor* (1995), and *Konikar Ramdhenu* (2003), has continued to explore themes of displacement, social injustice, and the enduring strength of the human spirit. His characters are often women, children, the elderly—those left unheard in the din of modern India.

Unlike many parallel cinema directors, Barua never drifted into abstraction. His films remained accessible, emotionally engaging, and rooted in realism. In 2005, he also directed *Maine Gandhi Ko Nahin Mara*, his only significant Hindi-language film, starring Anupam Kher in a powerful performance as a man suffering from dementia. The film used personal memory loss as a metaphor for India's fading moral compass—a striking theme for a filmmaker who has always been quietly political.

Jahnu Barua has received 12 National Film Awards, including multiple Best Regional Film and Best Director honours. He was awarded the Padma Shri in 2003 and the Padma Bhushan in 2015. His films have been screened at festivals in Berlin, Montreal, Moscow, and Tokyo. Through his cinema, the unseen villages of Assam are not only seen—they are also immortalised.

কাবলিওয়ালা

Tapan Sinha

Unobtrusive Excellence

(2 October 1924–15 January 2009)

Tapan Sinha crafted Bengali cinema with a similar emotional clarity as Barua's—but with a craftsman's range that defied easy categorisation. For decades, Sinha shaped Indian cinema with stories that were as technically accomplished as they were emotionally resonant, working in multiple languages—Bengali, Hindi, Oriya—and across genres.

Born in 1924 in Kolkata, Tapan Sinha began as a sound engineer at New Theatres, the famed studio that had once employed Bimal Roy and P.C. Barua. It was during a stint in England at Pinewood Studios, where he was exposed to European cinema, particularly the works of Vittorio De Sica and Carol Reed, that Sinha's aesthetics began to take shape. Returning to India, he chose to direct rather than remain behind the scenes.

His debut, *Ankush* (1954), showed his technical finesse and deep empathy for working-class struggles, but it was *Kabuliwala* (1957)—based on Tagore's short story—that cemented his reputation. Sinha's gift was not just adaptation—it was translation: of literature into cinema, of sentiment into structure. He would go on to make a remarkable variety of films: *Kshudhita Pashan* (based on Tagore's ghost story) (1960), *Hatey Bazarey* (a study in political and moral compromise) (1967), *Apanjan* (an unflinching look at youth disillusionment, later remade by Gulzar as *Mere Apne*) (1968), and *Safed Haathi* (1978), a beloved children's film in Hindi. With *Ek Doctor Ki Maut* (1990), based loosely on the life of Dr. Subhash Mukhopadhyay—who pioneered IVF in India but was shunned by the establishment—Sinha delivered a stinging critique of institutional indifference and intellectual isolation. The film won multiple National Awards, and remains one of Indian cinema's most scathing indictments of how brilliance is punished.

Sinha received 19 National Film Awards, multiple international recognitions, and the Dadasaheb Phalke Award in 2006. He was also awarded the Padma Shri, though never quite accorded the same stature as contemporaries like Satyajit Ray or Mrinal Sen—perhaps because his style was too subtle to be labelled, too sincere to be fashionable. In stories of teachers, doctors, migrants, rebels, and dreamers, Tapan Sinha built a cinema of enduring relevance and immense heart.

মৃণাল দা

Mrinal Sen

Cinema, Too, Is a Weapon.

(14 May 1923–30 December 2018)

Storming through cinema like a pamphlet fluttering in the wind—urgent, restless, and unafraid to tear the frame apart, Mrinal Sen looked forward—toward a political horizon, a promised revolution, or its bitter failure.

Born in Faridpur (Bangladesh), Mrinal Sen came of age in a world shaped by imperial collapse, famine, the ideological struggle, and the ferment of ideas around him—Marxism, anti-colonialism, modernist literature. He began as a film theorist and cultural critic, obsessed with Soviet cinema, Italian neorealism, and the French New Wave. He turned to direction with the understanding that cinema could be not only art, but argument.

His first film, *Raat Bhore* (1955), a conventional love story, passed largely unnoticed, but with *Baishey Shravana* (1960), a tragic love story set against the Bengal famine of 1943, Sen found his voice. In *Akash Kusum* (1965), he took a scathing look at middle-class aspirations, and with *Bhuvan Shome* (1969), starring Utpal Dutt as a bureaucrat undergoing a moral awakening in rural Gujarat, Sen entered the annals of New Indian Cinema. That film, financed by the Film Finance Corporation, is often cited as the moment parallel cinema officially took flight in India. Sen's defining work came in the '70s amidst Bengal's Naxalite movement and urban disillusionment: his Calcutta Trilogy—*Interview* (1971), *Calcutta 71* (1972), and *Padatik* (1973)—a series of fractured, semi-experimental films that blended narrative, documentary, and Brechtian technique to depict a city seething with class tension, moral compromise, and revolutionary angst. Often seen as part of the Ray-Ghatak-Sen trinity, unlike Ray or Ghatak, Sen always foregrounded history as ideology. In later films like *Ek Din Pratidin* (1979), *Kharij* (1982), and *Khandhar* (1984), his tone mellowed, but never softened.

Mrinal Sen won 13 National Film Awards, numerous international awards, including the Jury Prize at Cannes, Silver Bear at Berlin, and Golden Hugo at Chicago, and was awarded the Padma Bhushan in 1981 and the Dadasaheb Phalke Award in 2005.

In every cut, confrontation, and disjointed narrative, Mrinal Sen reminded us that the purpose of art is not to change the world—it is to remind us that the world must be changed.

কালপুরুষ
UTTARA
A film by

Buddhadeb Dasgupta

Onscreen Surrealist Poetry

(11 February 1944–10 June 2021)

If Sen's cinema marched with slogans, Buddhadeb Dasgupta's drifted like a dream across misty fields, empty train stations, and surreal visions of a country losing its way. Where Sen confronted politics head-on, Dasgupta painted reality as it felt—fractured, lyrical, often absurd. Watching a Dasgupta film is like waking up from a strange, beautiful sleep and remembering only the ache of what was lost.

Born in Purulia and raised in a middle-class Bengali family steeped in poetry and philosophy, Dasgupta trained as an economist. Inspired by European masters like Bresson and Tarkovsky, he turned to cinema, beginning with documentaries, where his ability to observe without intruding became quickly apparent. His first fiction feature, *Dooratwa* (1978), was a minimal, meditative story about alienation in the aftermath of the Naxalite movement. Clearly ahead of its time, its formal restraint and philosophical undertow set him apart.

In the '80s and '90s, Dasgupta's vision fully blossomed. *Neem Annapurna* (1979), *Grihajuddha* (1982), and *Andhi Gali* (1984) were all deeply political, but quietly so—eschewing rhetoric for mood, and ideology for allegory. Then came *Bagh Bahadur* (1989), a haunting tale of a village performer who paints himself as a tiger and dances to keep an ancient ritual alive.

In *Charachar* (1993), a bird seller confronts the futility of his trade in a world that cages not just animals but people. In *Uttara* (2000), two men duel endlessly with swords in the shadow of a rising tide of religious extremism. *Swapner Din* (2004), *Kaalpurush* (2005), and *Anwar Ka Ajab Kissa* (2013) all featured solitary wanderers—half in this world, half in memory—searching for love, justice, or simply a place to belong.

Buddhadeb Dasgupta won five National Film Awards for Best Director, multiple National Awards for Best Feature Film, and international honours at Venice, Berlin, Locarno, and Cairo. He was awarded the Padma Shri in 2007. He was also an acclaimed poet, with several collections to his name, and he often said he made films to 'write with light what could not be said in verse.' In his strange, surreal landscapes, the absurdity of the everyday found its most elegant chronicler.

I MADE FILMS BECAUSE I WANTED TO MAKE FILMS. I DIDN'T DO IT WITH THE INTENTION OF GIVING THE AUDIENCE A MESSAGE. THE ACT OF MAKING A FILM IS A SOCIAL ACT.

Mani Kaul

Cinema Minus the Melodrama

(25 December 1944–6 July 2011)

Unlike Dasgupta's poetry-turned-cinema, Mani Kaul turned cinema into pure abstraction. Kaul dismantled the very idea of narrative, breaking time, voice, space, and structure into elemental forms. His films don't follow a story—they drift, repeat, circle back, and often refuse to end.

Born Rabindranath Kaul in Jodhpur into a Kashmiri Pandit family, Kaul trained in direction at FTII under Ritwik Ghatak. Deeply influenced by Indian classical music, modernist literature, and avant-garde European filmmakers like Robert Bresson and Andrei Tarkovsky, Kaul's debut feature, *Uski Roti* (1969), adapted from a Mohan Rakesh story, was a landmark in Indian experimental cinema. The film, about a woman who waits every day for her indifferent husband at a dusty roadside, used non-professional actors, dislocated time, and flat, diffused lighting to create an experience closer to sculpture than storytelling.

He questioned cinema's obsession with climax, its addiction to drama, its insistence on resolution. In *Duvidha* (1973), based on a Rajasthani folktale about a ghost who takes the form of a woman's absent husband, Kaul stripped the story of all melodrama. The film won the National Film Award for Best Direction and remains one of the most singular interpretations of Indian folklore on film. Through the '70s and '80s, Kaul created a series of genre-defying works: *Satah Se Uthta Aadmi* (1980), *Dhrupad* (1982), *Nazar* (1991)—each drawing from poetry, music, and art. *Dhrupad*, a documentary on the musical form, is practically a visual raga. *Nazar*, inspired by Dostoevsky's *The Meek One*, is a film of silences and stares, where every movement feels like a brushstroke. Kaul also made television serials like *Idiot* (based on Dostoevsky's novel) and taught at various institutions, including FTII, Harvard, and Jamia Millia.

Mani Kaul received the Filmfare Critics Award, four National Film Awards, and widespread recognition across global film festivals. He also co-founded the Yukt Film Cooperative and inspired an entire generation of filmmakers and cinematographers. In his cinema, time isn't just felt—it expands, echoes, and transforms. To walk into a Mani Kaul film is to leave behind plot and enter the meditative space of light, breath, and silence.

WAVES OF REVOLUTION
A TIME TO RISE

Anand Patwardhan

Through an Unflinching Lens

(18 February 1950–)

Anand Patwardhan's films are not traditional stories—they are indictments, elegies, courtrooms, and battlefields, asking questions, not gently or metaphorically, but plainly: Why are we so silent? Why do we forget? Why do we look away?

Born in Bombay into a family of civil servants and writers, Patwardhan's filmmaking emerged from activism—street protests, slum movements, and anti-emergency agitation. His earliest work, *Waves of Revolution* (1974), was a handheld chronicle of the Bihar Student Movement led by Jayaprakash Narayan. Made secretly during the Emergency, it circulated underground, never officially released. His subsequent films charted a parallel history of post-Independence India—as felt in the voices of the dispossessed, the displaced, and the defiant.

Bombay: Our City (1985) documented the lives of Mumbai's slum dwellers and their fight against demolition drives. *Ram Ke Naam* (1992), his most explosive work, examined the rise of Hindutva extremism and the events leading up to the demolition of the Babri Masjid. One of the most politically potent Indian documentaries ever made, screened across universities, street corners, and activist spaces, TV channels refused to touch it. In *War and Peace* (2002), he tackled nuclear nationalism in the aftermath of the Pokhran and Chagai nuclear tests, juxtaposing India and Pakistan's arms race with the cost of jingoism. In *Father, Son and Holy War* (1995), he delved into the intersection of masculinity, communal violence, and sexual repression. His later work, *Jai Bhim Comrade* (2011), took 14 years to make and exposed caste atrocities against Dalits with searing poetry and precision. Patwardhan has routinely battled censorship boards, legal threats, and political opposition, yet his work has endured. He refuses to fictionalise, to soften, or to compromise. His aesthetic, too, is raw, observational, often eschewing voice-of-God narration for direct testimonies.

He has won more than 30 international awards, including the National Award for Best Investigative Film, Best Non-Feature Film, and Best Political Film across various years. His work has been screened at Cannes, Toronto, Berlin, and International Documentary Film Festival Amsterdam (IDFA), and he received the Lifetime Achievement Award from the Mumbai International Film Festival in 2019. In a country that often prefers silence, Anand Patwardhan never stops raising his voice.

JUSTICE
LIKE A WAR
A film by Deepa Dhanraj
THIRD
KOLKATA
PEOPLE'S
FILM
FESTIVAL
WE HAVE
NOT COME
HERE TO DIE
TRAILER LAUNCH

Deepa Dhanraj

The Pulse of Collaboration

(18 October 1953–)

If Anand Patwardhan films protest with the urgency of a frontline journalist, Deepa Dhanraj films it with the intimacy of someone within the struggle. Her cinema sits down with rural women, listens, translates rage into reason, and turns the act of filmmaking itself into a political alliance.

Born in 1953 in Hyderabad, Deepa Dhanraj began her career in the late '70s when few women in India were making films—let alone ones about caste, patriarchy, poverty, and resistance. She was self-taught, motivated not by film school but by the emerging feminist movement and her political consciousness. In 1980, she co-founded the Yugantar Film Collective, one of India's first feminist film groups. Together, they created films that weren't just about women—they were made with them, often in active dialogue with the communities being represented.

Her early documentaries—*Molkarin* (1981), *Tambaku Chaakila Oob Ali* (1982), and *Idhi Katha Matramena* (1983)—focused on domestic workers, tobacco factory women, and the everyday violence of unpaid labour. Her landmark film, *Something Like a War* (1991), exposed the coercive logic of India's population control programs, particularly the sterilisation of poor women, stripping their reproductive rights. It was as emotionally wrenching as it was intellectually precise—and is one of the most important feminist documentaries made in India. In later years, Dhanraj continued to focus on gender, health, and democracy. *The Advocate* (2007) chronicled the work of a Dalit lawyer fighting for social justice. *Invoking Justice* (2011) offered a compelling portrait of Muslim women's courts in Tamil Nadu, upending assumptions about Islamic jurisprudence.

Dhanraj never speaks for her subjects—she lets them speak, and listens without framing them as victims. Her collaborations often span years, and she treats consent and co-authorship as integral to the filmmaking process. She's won multiple international awards, including at IDFA, Yamagata, and Bangalore International Film Festival, and has been widely celebrated in academic, feminist, and development circles. Her influence on feminist documentary filmmaking in India is profound and ongoing. In her cinema, resistance speaks—not in slogans, but in the steady, clear voice of a woman telling her story.

Saba Dewan

Stories that History Tried to Erase

If Deepa Dhanraj brings the sharp light of activism to the margins, Saba Dewan's lens linger on the performers, dancers, and courtesans who occupy society's shadowlands—seen but unseen, desired but denied. Her cinema is political, yes, but also sensuous and haunted, infused with music, memory, and mourning.

Born in Delhi, trained at the Mass Communication Research Centre (MCRC) at Jamia Millia Islamia, she is part of a generation of filmmakers who believe in cinema as a cultural intervention. But unlike her peers who adopt a frontal, documentary style, Dewan chooses a more elliptical path—using performance, song, and slowness as tools to reveal the structures of patriarchy, class, and stigma.

Her early works—*Nasoor* (1991), *Dharmayuddha* (1989), and *Barf* (1997)—tackled communal violence, identity, and state brutality. But it was her turn toward the world of female performers that gave her cinema its distinctive voice. In *Delhi-Mumbai-Delhi* (2006), *Naach* (2008), and *The Other Song* (2009), Dewan constructed a loose, meditative trilogy that explored the lives of women dancers and singers—nautch girls, bar dancers, and *tawaifs*—who have long been objects of fascination, shame, and erasure. In *The Other Song*, perhaps her most celebrated film, Dewan sets out to find the forgotten women who once sang *thumris* in Benaras. The film begins with a single archival recording of a *tawaif's* voice and becomes an excavation—not just of music and memory, but of India's own fractured relationship with pleasure, gender, and caste. She traces how once-revered courtesans became social pariahs in post-colonial India, as nationalism and respectability converged to erase their legacy. The film is part travelogue, part lament, part cultural thesis—and entirely original. *Tawaifnama* (2019), Dewan's book, is a sweeping, multi-generational narrative of a community of courtesans in Banaras, written with the same care and lyricism as her films.

Saba Dewan has shown her work at Berlin, Yamagata, India Habitat Centre, and numerous academic and feminist forums. She is drawn to those who live in the half-light—not quite seen, not quite erased. In that half-light, Saba Dewan continues to find her poetry, her politics, and her power.

CHAUTHI
KOOT
ANHEY GHORHEY DA DAAN
(BITTER CHESTNUT)
KHANAUR

Gurvinder Singh

Introspection, Minimalism, Atmosphere

Stepping into the stark daylight of Punjab's fields—still and sun-baked—Gurvinder Singh's cinema never rushes. It listens, watching how people walk, pause, eat, and grieve, and in that slowness, it captures the ache—of displacement, of agrarian loss, of the quiet violence that unfolds far from the headlines.

Having studied at the National Institute of Design (NID), Ahmedabad, and later trained in direction at the FTII, Gurvinder Singh's cinema is shaped by long conversations with the soil, the wind, and the people of rural Punjab. His debut feature *Anhe Ghore Da Daan (Alms for a Blind Horse,* 2011), based on Gurdial Singh's novel, was an audacious, minimalist meditation on caste, labour, and resistance. Shot in grainy, poetic black-and-white, the film follows a day in the life of a Dalit family after a fellow villager's home is razed. Nothing dramatic happens, yet everything does. Oppression simmers in gestures, glances, and absences. There is no background score—only the ambient sound of carts, breaths, and wind. The film won the National Award for Best Direction and Best Cinematography, and premiered at the Venice Film Festival—marking Gurvinder Singh as one of the most distinctive new voices in Indian cinema.

His second feature, *Chauthi Koot (The Fourth Direction,* 2015), based on short stories by Waryam Singh Sandhu, turned to Punjab's insurgency years. Rather than depicting militants or security forces, Singh focuses on ordinary people caught in the crosshairs—two men taking a train ride, a family hiding their dog's bark out of fear. Fear is ambient, thick, and strangely banal. The film, which screened at Cannes (Un Certain Regard) and won the National Film Award for Best Punjabi Film, is not about action but atmosphere.

In his later work, including *Khanaur (Bitter Chestnut,* 2019), Singh continued to explore marginality—this time among the youth of Bir, Himachal Pradesh, caught between modern aspirations and traditional stagnation.

Gurvinder Singh has resisted the pull of commercial cinema, stating clearly that his films are not for escapism but for introspection. And in his work, a wounded land speaks louder than any script ever could.

THE SCREENPLAY KEEPS CHANGING AS I GROW OLDER AND YOUR IDEAS CHANGE AS YOU HAVE NEW EXPERIENCES, SO IT COMPLETELY CHANGED AS TIME WENT BY.

Payal Kapadia

Dissolving Dream and Documentary

(4 January 1986–)

Though Payal Kapadia's journey as a filmmaker is just beginning, she has already announced herself as a bold new voice, equally meditative and defiant. Her cinema is quiet but never still, pulsing with resistance, tenderness, and a search for what is lost—between people, inside memory, and through time.

Payal trained in direction at the FTII—an artistic crucible and a bureaucratic battleground—where her voice was forged. During the student protests in 2015 against the government's appointment of a controversial chairman, Kapadia was one of the most vocal participants. In that charged atmosphere of resistance, surveillance, and solidarity, the seeds of her cinema took root.

Her first short films—*Afternoon Clouds* (2017) and *And What Is the Summer Saying* (2018)—already displayed a formal daring that is rare in Indian cinema, blurring the lines between fiction and documentary, dream and document. *Summer Saying*, in particular, is a haunting portrait of longing, folklore, and gendered silences in rural Maharashtra. Its blend of whispered voiceover and intimate images is unlike anything else in the Indian short film landscape. But it was her debut feature, *A Night of Knowing Nothing* (2021), that truly catapulted her onto the global stage. Framed as a series of letters written by a young woman to a lover who has left FTII, the film is a found-footage archive of India's political and emotional turbulence. We hear her voice, but never see her. What we see instead are protests, empty hostels, masked faces, and flickering candles—moments suspended in time. The film premiered at Cannes 2021 (Directors' Fortnight) and won the prestigious L'Œil d'or (Golden Eye) for Best Documentary.

Payal has since been hailed as one of the most important new voices in world cinema. Her second feature, *All We Imagine As Light* (2024), became the first Indian film in three decades to compete in the main competition at the Cannes Film Festival, where it received standing ovations and widespread critical praise. Her style—intimate, slow, poetic—remains distinctly her own. In her world, where love is rebellion, memory is resistance, and silence is never neutral, cinema feels like a quiet revolution already underway.

THE ELEPHANT

Kartiki Gonsalves

Turning Reality into Fable

(2 November 1986–)

Where most filmmakers build a body of work before finding the global stage, Kartiki Gonsalves stepped into the light with her very first film—*The Elephant Whisperers*—and, in doing so, brought Indian documentary storytelling to the Academy Awards podium for the first time. Kartiki used the gaze of a wide-eyed elephant calf to remind the world of empathy. Growing up in the Nilgiri Hills, a region rich with wildlife, tribal cultures, and lush, untamed beauty, Kartiki's naturalist father nurtured her early fascination with animals and the outdoors. She studied photography and visual communication and worked as a nature and travel photographer before turning to filmmaking.

The Elephant Whisperers (2022), a 41-minute short documentary produced by Guneet Monga, follows Bomman and Bellie, a couple from the indigenous Kattunayakan tribe who care for two orphaned elephant calves, Raghu and Ammu, in Tamil Nadu's Mudumalai Tiger Reserve. What begins as a wildlife story soon becomes something more intimate. Gonsalves allows their world to unfold slowly—feeding rituals, bath time, bedtime snuggles, and moments of play—without commentary or lecturing. Instead, there is light, laughter, routine, and the unspoken bond between humans and animals, caretakers and the wild. The couple's story—marked by personal loss and quiet resilience—intertwines with the elephants' journey, creating a tapestry of care and coexistence that moved audiences worldwide. Without preaching about climate change or biodiversity, the film shows what happens when you treat nature as kin. It became the first Indian documentary to win an Academy Award—taking home the Oscar for Best Documentary Short Film in 2023. Kartiki was immediately hailed as a major new talent in nonfiction cinema. She was appointed as an Elephant Family Champion and featured in the TIME100 Impact Awards. But she remains grounded in her larger mission: using visual storytelling to foster empathy—for wildlife, indigenous communities, and the fragile ecosystems they share.

Showing love—not just human love, but the love that flows between species, between lives that aren't considered equal but very much are, *The Elephant Whisperers* gently, reverently, and with tenderness crossed continents.

THE EARTH MATTERS TO ALL OF US. DON'T JUST DRIVE TO WORK, LOOK AROUND YOU, SEE THE BIRDS AND TREES, AND IF THERE'S SOMETHING GOING WRONG, SET IT RIGHT.

Mike Pandey

An Advocate for the Endangered Wild

If Kartiki has showed us the bond between humans and elephants with lyrical tenderness, then Mike Pandey has been sounding the alarm about all that we risk losing—from whale sharks to forests, from rare birds to entire ecosystems. Where most filmmakers document wildlife for beauty, Pandey films it as a plea.

Born in Kenya and raised in India, Mike grew up surrounded by wildlife. His early years were spent in the forests of Bihar, where his father was a forest officer. That intimacy with nature never left him. After studying at the FTII and training in the UK and the US, Pandey returned to India determined to make films that not only showcased wildlife but also protected it.

He began in the '80s when wildlife filmmaking in India was still a rarity, focusing on endangered species and conservation issues, and connecting the plight of the animal to human responsibility. *The Last Migration* (1994), about the disappearing habitat of elephants, and *Vanishing Giants* (1996), brought attention to India's troubled relationship with its largest land mammal. But it was *Shores of Silence: Whale Sharks in India* (2000) that became a landmark. Filmed off the coast of Gujarat, it exposed the brutal killing of whale sharks—then classified as fish and unprotected by Indian law. The film was responsible for a complete policy overhaul. India declared the whale shark as a protected species soon after the film was aired, thanks to public pressure. *In Broken Wings* (2002), he focused on the critically endangered vultures of India, documenting how the use of veterinary drugs had decimated populations and upset ecological balance. Again, the drug in question, diclofenac, was banned for veterinary use.

Mike has won three Green Oscars (Wildscreen Panda Awards)—the highest honour in international wildlife filmmaking—alongside National Film Awards, Earth Vision Tokyo, and other global accolades. More importantly, he's helped build a culture of conservation awareness in India. He also hosted and produced *Earth Matters,* one of Doordarshan's longest-running environmental series, and he continues to mentor young conservationists and campaign for environmental legislation. Film by film, he became the wilderness's most devoted storyteller—not to celebrate its grandeur, but to plead for its survival.

I PLAY FOR A LIVING...
MY HOPE IS WE BROKE SO MANY RULES WE CREATED A NEW RULE.

M. Night Shyamalan

Indian Roots That Echo

(6 August 1970–)

Carrying a legacy where Indian ancestry met American anxiety, where ghosts whispered not from forests but from within homes, corridors, and family histories, M. Night Shyamalan's cinema is a hall of mirrors—reflective, eerie, and about the search for meaning in the most ordinary places.

Born Manoj Nelliyattu Shyamalan in Puducherry as the son of Indian doctors who emigrated to the United States, he grew up in suburban Pennsylvania—with a deep undercurrent of otherness that would infuse his films. He began making home movies at age eight and went on to study filmmaking at the Tisch School of the Arts, where he adopted the middle name 'Night'. Though his debut, *Praying with Anger* (1992), and second film, *Wide Awake* (1998), were modest, *The Sixth Sense* (1999) launched him into the stratosphere. The psychological thriller, starring Bruce Willis and Haley Joel Osment, became a global phenomenon thanks to its iconic twist ending. It earned six Academy Award nominations, including Best Director and Best Original Screenplay, making Shyamalan an overnight sensation.

In the years that followed, Shyamalan became known as the master of the twist. *Unbreakable* (2000), *Signs* (2002), and *The Village* (2004) further cemented his fascination with the supernatural and the psychological, but always through the lens of deeply personal stories. The 2000s brought backlash. Films like *Lady in the Water* (2006), *The Happening* (2008), and *The Last Airbender* (2010) were widely panned. Critics accused him of hubris, of self-indulgence, of having lost his touch. But Shyamalan remained undeterred. He returned to smaller budgets, leaned into horror and thriller with renewed clarity, and re-emerged stronger than ever with *The Visit* (2015), *Split* (2016), and *Glass* (2019)—completing his *Unbreakable* trilogy and restoring his reputation as a master of tension and mood.

Shyamalan has not won an Oscar but has received numerous awards and nominations, including Saturn Awards, Empire Awards, and a BAFTA nomination. He's been celebrated for redefining the American thriller and horror genre for a generation, and his work has influenced countless filmmakers worldwide. In his world, fear is never just fear. It's a doorway—to truth, to revelation, and sometimes, to redemption.

ভাবো ,ভাবো,ভাবা
প্র্যাকটিস করো।

Ritwik Ghatak

The Brutal Realism of Cultural Trauma

(4 November 1925–6 February 1976)

If Ray gave cinema its humanism, then Ritwik Ghatak gave it its howl. His films were cries of anguish, fractured visions of a land, and a people broken by Partition, alienation, and loss.

Born in Dhaka, Ghatak came of age amidst the trauma of Partition, and that rupture became the epicentre of his work. He trained in theatre and literature before turning to cinema, and his films are as much about performance and language as they are about image.

Ghatak's early work struggled to find commercial or critical acceptance. His debut *Nagarik* (1952), often considered the first film of Indian art cinema, wasn't released in his lifetime. His next films—*Ajantrik* (1958), about a man and his decaying car, and *Bari Theke Paliye* (1959), about a runaway child—were radical and emotionally unsettling. But it was in the '60s that Ghatak created his trilogy of cultural trauma: *Meghe Dhaka Tara* (1960), *Komal Gandhar* (1961), and *Subarnarekha* (1965). These films, which explored the lives of refugees in post-Partition Bengal, fused myth with realism, pathos with political critique, and personal loss with national fracture. In *Meghe Dhaka Tara (The Cloud-Capped Star)*, the protagonist Nita—a self-sacrificing sister supporting her disintegrating family—is perhaps the most tragic figure in Indian cinema. Her final scream, '*Dada, ami banchte chai!*' ('Brother, I want to live!'), still echoes across generations.

Komal Gandhar dealt with divided theatre groups as metaphors for the divided nation, while *Subarnarekha*, arguably his bleakest, traced the inexorable decline of a refugee family through themes of incest, poverty, and suicide. Ghatak's later years were marked by struggle. He directed only eight feature films, worked intermittently at FTII where he mentored future legends like Kumar Shahani and Mani Kaul, and battled chronic alcoholism and depression.

Ghatak was awarded the Padma Shri in 1970 and the National Film Award for Best Story for *Jukti Takko Aar Gappo* (1977), his last, self-reflexive film in which he played a drunken intellectual wandering through a broken nation. His influence on Indian cinema, however, is immeasurable. Through his pain, Ghatak gave Indian cinema its fiercest conscience and its most unforgettable ache.

Dibakar Banerjee

The Middle Cinema Satirist

(21 June 1969–)

In a landscape of heroes and villains, Banerjee populates his stories with cynics, hustlers, and people hanging by the thread of morality. With his dark humour, fractured narratives, and urban decay, Banerjee has become one of the most incisive chroniclers of post-liberalisation India.

Born in Delhi, Banerjee grew up watching Ray and '80s Doordarshan serials, absorbing the quiet rhythm of the middle class. Working in advertising shaped the grammar of his films—compact, layered, and charged with subversion. His debut feature, *Khosla Ka Ghosla* (2006), was a small-budget satire made with character actors and a script as rooted in Delhi as the DDA flats it lovingly mocked. It was a sleeper hit and signalled Banerjee's arrival as someone who could turn local anxieties into national resonance.

But it was *Oye Lucky! Lucky Oye!* (2008), which cemented his style—a manic, stylish, genre-bending film about a charming thief from West Delhi. Inspired by the real-life exploits of Bunty Chor, the film veered from absurdist comedy to class critique, tracing a restless young man's hunger for the good life through stolen TVs and sedans. With *Love Sex Aur Dhokha* (2010), Banerjee blew up the frame altogether. Shot entirely on surveillance cameras, handheld footage, and CCTV-style setups, the film was a moral gut punch—raw, uncomfortable, and groundbreaking—arguably the most important Indian film of that year.

Banerjee followed it with *Shanghai* (2012), a political thriller that turned development dreams into Kafkaesque nightmares. It cast Abhay Deol, Emraan Hashmi, and Kalki Koechlin in a sinister tale of urban redevelopment and bureaucratic complicity. As with most of his work, the city is not a setting—it's a character, oppressive and seductive. He has also directed acclaimed short films like *Star* in *Bombay Talkies* (2013), each an experimental, elliptical dive into fractured psyches.

Dibakar Banerjee has received two National Film Awards, including Best Feature Film and Best Popular Film. He remains a key voice in India's 'middle cinema'—not quite mainstream, not quite arthouse, but always biting. With every sharp cut and morally ambiguous character, he does just that—unsettling the viewer, one satire at a time.

LAGAAN

Ashutosh Gowariker

The Sincerity of Epic Storytelling

(15 February 1964–)

Ashutosh Gowariker has reintroduced earnestness—long-form epics that believed in history, nationhood, and decency. In a post-liberalisation Bollywood moving rapidly toward gloss, he reintroduced audiences to gravitas. Born in Mumbai, Gowariker began as an actor, appearing in films like *Naam* and television shows like *Circus*. His directorial debut, *Pehla Nasha* (1993), passed unnoticed, and it was only with his third film that he struck gold—and history.

Lagaan (2001) was a phenomenon. A sports movie set in colonial India about a ragtag group of villagers challenging their British oppressors to a game of cricket, it combined every seemingly unworkable element—British actors, Bhojpuri-accented Hindi, a nearly four-hour runtime—and somehow turned it into one of the most loved Indian films of all time. Produced by Aamir Khan, the film became India's official entry to the Oscars and was nominated for Best Foreign Language Film, only the third Indian film in history to receive that honour. But *Lagaan* wasn't just a success—it was a turning point. It reignited faith in historical fiction, in the ensemble epic, in films rooted in Indian soil but narratively ambitious. The villagers, their dusty fields, their musical camaraderie, their David-and-Goliath fight against the empire—it all struck a chord in an India balancing its rural backbone with its urban dreams. Gowariker followed *Lagaan* with *Swades* (2004), his most quietly powerful film. Starring Shah Rukh Khan as a NASA engineer who returns to India and reconnects with his roots, the film asked not just what progress meant—but who got left behind. It was intimate, idealistic, and deeply moving.

His later ventures into historical epics—*Jodhaa Akbar* (2008) and *Mohenjo Daro* (2016)—met with varying responses. *Jodhaa Akbar,* a lavish romance between a Mughal emperor and a Rajput princess, was praised for its grandeur and won several Filmfare Awards, including Best Director. *Mohenjo Daro*, however, was less successful, criticised for historical liberties and a dated tone. More than a director, he's become synonymous with large-scale, emotionally anchored Indian cinema. In the generous, earnest, expansive heart of Gowariker's cinema, time doesn't drag—it deepens.

RGV
WHEN SOMEONE IS UP THERE AND HE DESERVES TO BE UP THERE, TRY TO LEARN FROM WHAT HE HAS ACHIEVED.

Ram Gopal Varma

The Vocabulary of Fear

(7 April 1962–)

Ram Gopal Varma has condensed cinema into a dark, throbbing underworld—lit by neon, scored by silence, and haunted by gunshots—transforming Indian filmmaking with a visceral, kinetic style that rewrote the grammar of genre.

Starting out by managing a video rental store, where he obsessively consumed films and internalised their rhythms, his obsession with craft, with angles, edits, and atmosphere, made him one of the most visually audacious filmmakers. Debuting with the Telugu film *Shiva* (1989), a gritty campus drama that turned violent youth politics into stylish action, the film, starring Nagarjuna, became a phenomenon and was later remade in Hindi.

But it was with *Satya* (1998) that Varma truly changed the course of Hindi cinema. Co-written with Saurabh Shukla and Anurag Kashyap, the film followed a migrant outsider who drifts into Mumbai's gang wars. There were no heroes here, no stars, no glamour—only moral greys and the claustrophobia of narrow stairwells, chawls, and bar-lit conspiracies. *Satya* redefined the gangster genre in India, launching the 'Mumbai noir' aesthetic that influenced a generation of filmmakers from Vishal Bhardwaj to Hansal Mehta. Varma followed it with *Kaun* (1999), a chilling psychological thriller made in a single location; *Company* (2002), a fictionalised account of the Dawood-Chhota Rajan split, and *Bhoot* (2003), one of the few Indian horror films that succeeded both critically and commercially. In each of these, he played with form—handheld cameras, offbeat casting, moody soundscapes—and brought a documentary immediacy to fiction.

At his peak, RGV was more than a director—he was a studio head, mentor, and cultural force. But his career has also been famously erratic. Varma's output in the late 2000s and 2010s became prolific but uneven—spawning everything from documentaries and experimental horror films to controversial political dramas and self-parodies. Ram Gopal Varma has won two National Film Awards, multiple Filmfare Awards, and is credited with modernising the visual language of Indian cinema—especially in crime, horror, and psychological drama. Few directors have fallen from grace as spectacularly, or shaped an entire era with such impact. Varma has made his cinema not always flawless, but always fearless.

TI ANI
AAKROS
DRISHTI
HAZA
JUNOON
DEV
TAMAS
DROH
KAAL
KI MAA
VIJETA

Govind Nihalani

The Lens and the Conscience

(19 December 1940–)

If RGV has prowled the underworld with stylised nihilism, Govind Nihalani has confronted it with moral fury. Nihalani's cinema was not entertainment but indictment, shaping the political and social landscape of Indian parallel cinema with a sense of emotional urgency.

Nihalani and his family migrated to India after Partition. He trained at the FTII, specialising in cinematography. He collaborated with Shyam Benegal, for whom he served as cinematographer on landmark films such as *Ankur* (1974), *Nishant* (1975), and *Manthan* (1976). It was only in 1980 that Nihalani stepped into the director's chair—with a film that would change the idiom of Indian political cinema. *Aakrosh* (1980), written by Vijay Tendulkar, tells the story of a silent tribal man accused of murder, whose muteness hides a deeper tragedy rooted in caste, power, and systemic abuse. The film didn't just resonate—it jolted. It won the National Film Award for Best Feature Film in Hindi, and Om Puri's haunting performance became one of the most enduring faces of India's marginalised.

Nihalani followed it with *Ardh Satya* (1983), his most iconic film, and certainly one of the finest in Indian cinema. Again featuring Om Puri in a career-defining role, the film explored the crumbling of an idealistic police officer caught between personal morality and institutional rot. It became emblematic of a generation's disillusionment with the state.

Throughout the '80s and '90s, Nihalani continued to direct films that wrestled with India's social fault lines. *Party* (1984) dissected the hypocrisy of urban intellectuals. *Tamas* (1988), a television miniseries based on Bhisham Sahni's novel about Partition, was a staggering achievement—bold, painful, and almost unbearably honest. It won several National Awards, including Best Director and Best Serial. Later works like *Drohkaal* (1994), about the moral toll of counterinsurgency, and *Hazaar Chaurasi Ki Maa* (1998), adapted from Mahasweta Devi's novel about Naxalism and motherhood, continued his engagement with political and psychological conflict. Govind Nihalani has received the Padma Shri. He also served as chair of various film institutions and remains a respected voice in debates around media ethics and state censorship. His cinema doesn't flinch, doesn't compromise, and never, ever looks away.

मैं एक ऐसा आदमी हूँ, जो हर चीज़
से प्यार करता हूँ।

Guru Dutt

The Melancholic Cinematic Poet

(9 July 1925–10 October 1964)

If Ray gave Indian cinema its intellect, and Raj Kapoor its heart, then Guru Dutt gave it its ache. His films are like old letters—creased, perfumed with longing, and too painful to read in one sitting.

Born Vasanth Kumar Shivashankar Padukone, he began as a choreographer and assistant director before directing his first film, *Baazi* (1951), for friend and producer Dev Anand. The film was a hit, and Guru Dutt became a name to watch.

What followed was something rarer than success: a body of work that turned personal despair into universal poetry. In *Jaal* (1952), *Aar Paar* (1954), and *Mr. & Mrs. 55* (1955), Dutt created stylish, sophisticated films that entertained, but with an undercurrent of melancholy. Then came *Pyaasa* (1957), one of the greatest films in Indian cinema. Dutt played Vijay, a struggling poet rejected by a materialistic world. It was semi-autobiographical, though he never claimed so, and every frame is drenched in yearning—his for love, for art, for redemption. *'Yeh duniya agar mil bhi jaaye toh kya hai'* became an existential sigh shared by generations.

His next masterpiece, *Kaagaz Ke Phool* (1959), was even more personal—and initially, a commercial failure. India's first in CinemaScope, it told the story of a fallen film director destroyed by the very industry that once worshipped him. After its rejection, he never officially directed a film again. Yet he remained an indelible presence—in *Chaudhvin Ka Chand* (1960), which he produced and acted in, and *Sahib Bibi Aur Ghulam* (1962), a tragic tale of decay and desire, directed by his protégé Abrar Alvi but widely believed to bear Dutt's directorial imprint. His heroines—Waheeda Rehman, Meena Kumari, Madhubala—were muses, the soul of a decaying world.

Guru Dutt died young, at just 39, in what was likely a suicide—though even in death, he left behind a mystery as elegantly tragic as his films. He was posthumously celebrated with retrospectives at Cannes, Venice, and the Cinematheque Française. Revered today as a cinematic poet, in every dimly lit frame, every sorrowful glance, Guru Dutt has etched a place in ours.

EK
GADDAAR
RAGHAVAN FILM
PRODUCED BY

Sriram Raghavan

Modern Indian Noir

(22 June 1963–)

If Guru Dutt painted noir with longing and lyricism, then Sriram Raghavan chisels it with a scalpel—seeking not your sympathy but attention, and once he has it, he twists the knife.

Growing up on a steady diet of pulp thrillers and the erratic genius of '70s Bollywood, Raghavan studied at the FTII, and his graduation film, *The Eight Column Affair* (1987), was already a whodunit, establishing a career template marked by misdirection, deception, and impeccable pacing.

He began in documentary and television—most notably *Raman Raghav: A City, A Killer* (1991), an eerie account of Mumbai's infamous serial murderer. His feature debut, *Ek Hasina Thi* (2004), starring Urmila Matondkar and Saif Ali Khan, announced him as a new kind of storyteller. A revenge thriller, the film was taut, stylish, and a revelation in a decade dominated by family sagas and bubblegum romances. Raghavan's next film, *Johnny Gaddaar* (2007), was pure pulp elegance, following a group of small-time hustlers as one of them tries to outplay the others. The film was wickedly self-aware, with every frame steeped in homage and irony. It wasn't a hit—but became a cult classic among noir aficionados. Then came *Badlapur* (2015), a brutal, brooding tale of vengeance with Varun Dhawan in a grim performance. Here, Raghavan blurred the moral lines between victim and aggressor, between justice and obsession. Critics praised its emotional complexity; audiences were shaken by its darkness.

But his masterpiece, *Andhadhun* (2018), about a blind pianist who may not be blind, a murder that may not be a murder, and a rabbit that might just be a red herring—the film is a genre-bending ride. Ayushmann Khurrana, Tabu, and Radhika Apte delivered career-best performances, winning three National Film Awards, including Best Hindi Film and Best Actor, making it a rare thriller to be a box office hit and a critical darling.

Raghavan, one of the finest genre filmmakers in India, is admired for his economy, wit, and refusal to moralise. He trusts his audience, keeps his characters flawed, and never wastes a shot. In his world, real is the first illusion—and betrayal the closest thing to truth.

I HAVE A FASCINATION FOR CARTOONS. NO MATTER HOW MANY TIMES 'TOM AND JERRY' FALL, YOU NEVER COMPLAIN, AND WATCH IT AGAIN.

Priyadarshan

Choreographed Chaos

(30 January 1957–)

If Raghavan's thrillers demand your attention, Priyadarshan's comedies ask only for your laughter—again and again. They burst onto the screen with chaos, confusion, and charm. Yet beneath the slapstick and mistaken identities lies a master of timing, structure, and adaptation. A Priyadarshan farce is a symphony of misunderstanding.

Beginning his career in Malayalam cinema, directing hit comedies, thrillers, and social dramas throughout the '80s and '90s, Priyadarshan worked with stars like Mohanlal and Sreenivasan to quickly become one of the most prolific and commercially successful directors in the South. His early films—*Boeing Boeing (1985), Kilukkam (1991), Thenmavin Kombathu (1994)*—were celebrated for their sharp wit, character depth, and narrative discipline.

His entry into Hindi cinema introduced Priyadarshan to a pan-Indian audience. His first major Hindi hit, *Hera Pheri* (2000), wasn't just a remake of his own Malayalam film *Ramji Rao Speaking*—it was a cultural reset. Starring Paresh Rawal, Akshay Kumar, and Suniel Shetty, the film became an enduring classic, quoted endlessly, rewatched obsessively. Rawal's portrayal of Baburao Ganpatrao Apte became one of Indian comedy's most beloved creations. Over the next decade, Priyadarshan became synonymous with ensemble comedies and chaotic climax scenes that often involved running, shouting, mistaken identities, and collapsing furniture—films like *Hungama* (2003), *Hulchul* (2004), *Garam Masala* (2005), *Bhagam Bhag* (2006), and *De Dana Dan* (2009). And yet, to pigeonhole Priyadarshan as just a comedy director would be to miss half the picture. His films like *Virasat* (1997)—a Hindi adaptation of *Thevar Magan* (1992)—and *Kanchivaram* (2008), a Tamil-language period drama about a silk weaver, reveal a director capable of emotional depth and political awareness. *Kanchivaram* won the National Film Award for Best Feature Film and remains one of his most personal, poignant works.

Priyadarshan has directed over 90 films across languages, won multiple National Awards, and received the Padma Shri in 2012. Few filmmakers in India have shown such fluency across genres, such longevity, and such consistent command over an audience's attention—whether through tears or laughter. The secret to comedy is to always take it seriously, a mantra he has diligently pursued—for well over four decades.

FARAA
OMERTÀ
CITYLIG

Hansal Mehta

Piercing the Core

(29 April 1968–)

Hansal Mehta dives into chaos for truth, finds purpose in discomfort. Mehta's cinema is not breezy—it is raw, questioning, and often deeply unsettling. His films ask: what happens to those whom society forgets, punishes, or scapegoats? In answering, Mehta has given contemporary Indian cinema some of its most piercing character studies.

Born in Mumbai, Mehta began his career in the '90s, making light comedies and food shows on television. His early films—*Jayate* (1999), *Dil Pe Mat Le Yaar* (2000), and *Chhal* (2002)—were competent but unremarkable. For a time, Mehta disappeared from the cinematic map, disillusioned with the industry's compromises. He returned a decade later—with a vengeance, and a voice. *Shahid* (2013), based on the real-life story of human rights lawyer Shahid Azmi, was the turning point. Starring Rajkummar Rao in a fearless, stripped-down performance, the film traced Azmi's transformation from riot-accused teenager to a lawyer who defended those branded as terrorists. The film earned Mehta the National Award for Best Direction, and Rao won Best Actor. More importantly, it marked the rebirth of a filmmaker who now had something to say—and wouldn't stop. He followed this with *City Lights* (2014), a bleak yet tender portrait of rural migration to urban anonymity, and *Aligarh* (2015), a hauntingly intimate account of a university professor persecuted for being gay. Manoj Bajpayee's portrayal of Prof. Siras—shy, poetic, lonely—remains one of Hindi cinema's most heartbreaking performances. In telling Siras's story, Mehta didn't sensationalise, he humanised. And that, perhaps, is his signature: the ability to bring dignity to the marginalised without turning them into martyrs. Then came *Scam 1992* (2020), the web series that blended financial jargon with Shakespearean ambition. It was stylised, tightly written, and grounded by Pratik Gandhi's phenomenal performance.

Now among the most respected voices in Indian independent and crossover cinema, Mehta continues to alternate between politically urgent cinema and more mainstream ventures, always tethered to the idea that personal stories are never just personal. And in that quest for understanding, Mehta has become not just a filmmaker—but a chronicler of India's difficult truths.

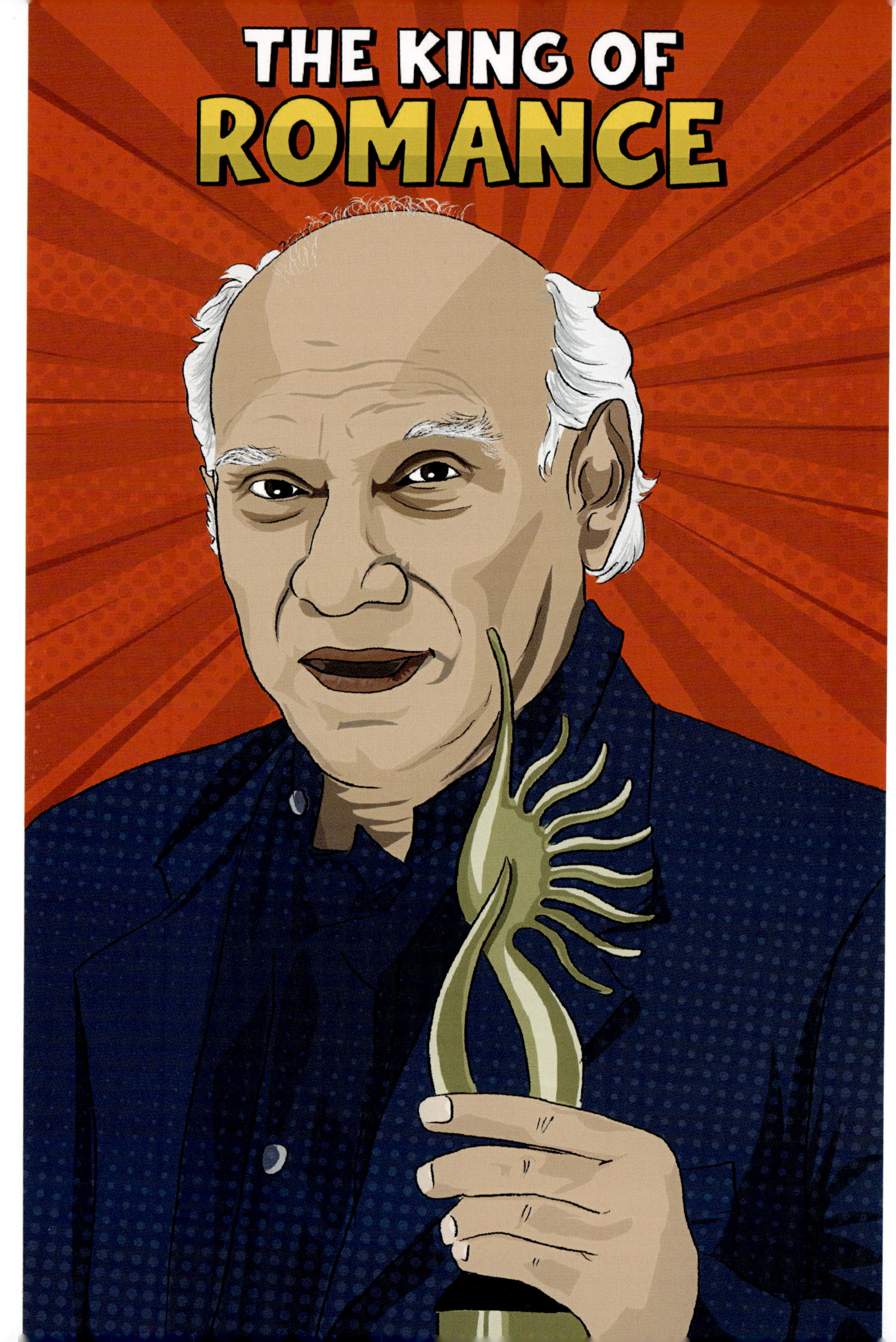
THE KING OF
ROMANCE

Yash Chopra

Cinema of Desire, Dignity, and Enduring Grace

(27 September 1932–21 October 2012)

Yash Chopra seduced India with romance—and then, slowly, showed how fragile even dreams could be. His cinema shimmered with chiffon and snow, but beneath was a steady pulse of emotional truth. Where others gave us fantasy, Chopra gave us feeling.

Born in Lahore, Yash Raj began working under his brother, the legendary B.R. Chopra. He directed *Dhool Ka Phool* (1959), a progressive drama about illegitimacy, and *Dharmputra* (1961), one of the first Hindi films to openly confront communal hatred.

In the '70s, Yash Chopra found his signature voice: romance layered with conflict. *Daag* (1973), *Kabhie Kabhie* (1976), and *Silsila* (1981) explored love not as a given, but as a risk, complicated by marriage, guilt, and memory. These films weren't just about roses and reunions. They were about choices made in moments of weakness, and the shadows those choices cast. *Silsila*, in particular, starring Amitabh Bachchan, Jaya Bachchan, and Rekha, mirrored real-life rumours, becoming a part of cultural memory—quiet, stylish, emotionally intelligent. In the '80s, Chopra shifted gears again, proving his versatility. *Chandni* (1989) brought back romance in an era dominated by action films. With its lush music, graceful heroine, and pastel palette, it redefined mainstream cinema and helped launch Sridevi into superstardom. Then came *Lamhe* (1991), a bold tale of an older man falling in love with the daughter of the woman he once loved. The late '90s and early 2000s brought perhaps his most iconic works: *Dil To Pagal Hai* (1997) and *Veer-Zaara* (2004). In *Veer-Zaara,* Chopra returned to the themes of cross-border love, sacrifice, and fate—marking his final directorial work and capping his career with a tribute to unity, compassion, and timeless love. In between, he nurtured countless careers—including directors like Aditya Chopra and Karan Johar.

Yash Chopra received eight Filmfare Awards for Best Director, the Dadasaheb Phalke Award in 2001, and the Padma Bhushan in 2005. He founded Yash Raj Films, one of the most powerful and influential studios in Indian cinema. He made films about relationships, and in those relationships—complicated, unspoken, impossible—Yash Chopra found his poetry.

तू ऐसे सौ SHER SINGH RANA को हरायेगा!
TU HAI AAG, MILKHA! OH, BAS TU BHAAG, MILKHA!
ZINDAGI JEENE KE DO HI TARIKE HOTE HAI... EK JO HO RAHA HAI HONE DO, BARDAASHT KARTE JAO. YA PHIR ZIMMEDARI UTHAO USSE BADALNE KI!
COLLEGE DI GATE DE IS TARAF HUM LIFE KO NACHATE HAI ... TE DUJI TARAF LIFE HUMKO NACHATI HAI
delhi-6

Rakeysh Omprakash Mehra

Revolution and Inner Demons

(7 July 1963–)

Rakeysh Omprakash Mehra's films are not about gentle longing but about fire: the fire of youth, of ideals, of memory reclaiming meaning.

Beginning as an ad filmmaker, Mehra's early foray into cinema, *Aks* (2001), was ambitious but uneven—featuring Amitabh Bachchan in a supernatural thriller that flirted with genre without quite landing. Then came *Rang De Basanti* (2006)—a film that didn't just connect with audiences; it galvanised them. The story of a group of college students who play Indian revolutionaries for a documentary and slowly begin to absorb their ideology, it became a cultural lightning rod. With a cast led by Aamir Khan, a searing soundtrack by A.R. Rahman, and non-linear storytelling, *Rang De Basanti* made history feel immediate and protest feel personal.

It wasn't just a film—it was a movement. Viewers marched with candles, quoted dialogues at rallies, and sang *Luka Chuppi* in vigils. It won the National Award for Best Popular Film and became India's official entry to the Oscars, cementing Mehra's status as a filmmaker of national consequence. He followed it with *Delhi-6* (2009), a more meditative and semi-autobiographical work about identity and belonging in the heart of Old Delhi. The film, though divisive, offered powerful metaphors—particularly its *kaala bandar* (black monkey) as a stand-in for societal paranoia and inner demons. Its soundtrack, again by Rahman, outlived the film's box office run. But it was *Bhaag Milkha Bhaag* (2013) that returned Mehra to critical and commercial acclaim. A biopic of the legendary sprinter Milkha Singh, played by Farhan Akhtar, the film traced not just athletic triumphs but the trauma of Partition and the resilience of the human spirit, earning Mehra the Filmfare Award for Best Director. His subsequent works, including *Mirzya* (2016) and *Toofaan* (2021), continued to explore themes of duality, redemption, and identity—though without the same cultural impact.

Mehra has been honoured with National Awards, Filmfare Awards, and is known for championing strong scripts, unconventional storytelling, and a deep engagement with the Indian conscience—past and present. And in that feeling—of rebellion, nostalgia, and unfinished dreams—Mehra has built a cinema that doesn't just entertain, but reminds.

S.S. Rajamouli

The Crescendo of Visual Storytelling

(10 October 1973–)

S.S. Rajamouli seizes the imagination, conjuring myth and might. His cinema isn't introspective—it's elemental. Mountains split, chains snap, eagles soar, and warriors leap across battlefields with thunder in their veins. And yet, beneath the spectacle lies something deeply Indian: a belief in heroism not as fantasy, but as destiny fulfilled.

Koduri Srisaila Sri Rajamouli grew up in a family steeped in storytelling. His father, K.V. Vijayendra Prasad, was a screenwriter, and together, father and son would reshape the landscape of Indian popular cinema. Rajamouli began in television and made his feature debut with *Student No.1* (2001), a modest Telugu-language success. But it was with *Magadheera* (2009), a reincarnation epic spanning centuries, that he announced the scale of his ambition—and his ability to deliver on it.

His films are not bound by genre. *Eega* (2012), a revenge drama in which a murdered man is reincarnated as a housefly, became a cult sensation for its outrageous premise and technical audacity. But it was the Baahubali duology—*Baahubali: The Beginning* (2015) and *Baahubali 2: The Conclusion* (2017)—that turned Rajamouli into a household name across India and among the diaspora. With its breathtaking world-building, iconic characters, and operatic narrative, the two-part saga became the highest-grossing Indian film series at the time. *Baahubali 2* shattered records and rewrote the rules for what a homegrown Indian fantasy epic could achieve—without any need for Western validation or crossover stars. Then came *RRR* (2022), a fictionalised bromance between two real-life freedom fighters, Komaram Bheem and Alluri Sitarama Raju. Blending historical fiction, superhero physics, and musical extravagance, the film exploded across the globe. It wasn't just a hit—it was a phenomenon. The song *Naatu Naatu* won the Academy Award for Best Original Song, a first for an Indian production. More importantly, RRR became a viral celebration of cinematic maximalism—praised by filmmakers from James Cameron to the Russo Brothers for its unapologetic, kinetic storytelling.

S.S. Rajamouli has won three National Film Awards, the Padma Shri (2023), and numerous global honours. His stories have gone far—beyond borders, beyond logic, and straight into the cinematic hall of legends.

HIDAYATKAR-E-AZAM
LIP KUMAR-NARGIS-RAJ KAPOOR
NDAZ
MOTHER INDIA

Mehboob Khan

The Roots of Grandeur

(9 September 1907–28 May 1964)

If Rajamouli's epics are a twenty-first-century spectacle of triumph and thunder, then Mehboob Khan was the one who first dreamt in widescreen before the frame even allowed it. Before there were VFX battles and global box office charts, there was *Mother India* (1957)—a film so grand, so rooted, and so defining that it came to represent the very soul of Indian cinema.

Mehboob Khan ran away from home and began his career as a bit player in silent films in Bombay. But his rise was meteoric. He directed his first feature, *Judgement of Allah*, in 1935, and soon developed a reputation for making socially engaged melodramas that tackled poverty, exploitation, and the complex moralities of the Indian family. By the '40s, with films like *Aurat* (1940) and *Roti* (1942), he was already pushing the limits of narrative scale and ideological engagement.

But it was *Mother India* (1957) that immortalised him. A remake of *Aurat*, this time with the benefit of colour, scope, and a maturing nation's emotional expectations, the film starred Nargis as Radha, the suffering-yet-unyielding matriarch of a rural family. The story was simple—of debt, drought, and sacrifice—but the film turned that simplicity into epic moral drama. It wasn't just a film about a mother; it was about the motherland. The final act—where Radha shoots her bandit son to preserve the law—was nothing short of national mythmaking. *Mother India* was the first Indian film to be nominated for the Academy Award for Best Foreign Language Film and remains one of the most iconic works in world cinema. Before *Mother India,* Khan had already created hits like *Andaz* (1949), a modern love triangle starring Raj Kapoor, Dilip Kumar, and Nargis, and *Aan* (1952), India's first Technicolor blockbuster—a swashbuckling romance that combined sword fights with social messaging.

Mehboob Khan won the Filmfare Award for Best Director and Best Picture, and was awarded the Padma Shri. He passed away just a few years after the release of *Mother India,* leaving behind a filmography that is compact but monumental. He placed cinema at the service of the nation—not as propaganda, but as prayer.

मैदान ए जंग में तलवार सिपाही के हाथ में दी जाती है मायूस आशिक़ के हाथ में नहीं।

K. Asif

Of Perfectionism and Timeless Love

(14 June 1922–9 March 1971)

If Mehboob Khan gave India its moral mother, then K. Asif gave it its tragic prince. Where *Mother India* was a cry of sacrifice and resilience, *Mughal-e-Azam* (1960) was a coronation—of cinema itself. Opulent, operatic, maddeningly perfectionist, and so soaked in splendour that it seemed less made than summoned.

Asif Karim arrived in Bombay with dreams far bigger than his modest beginnings. He directed his first film, *Phool* (1945), with some success, but it was *Mughal-e-Azam*—his life's obsession—that would consume his career, his finances, and ultimately define his legacy. He began working on it as early as 1944. The project was halted by financial constraints, recasting, political upheavals, and even Partition. Most other filmmakers would have abandoned it. Asif refused.

The film finally released in 1960, after over fifteen years of production. It had been shot in black and white, but its most iconic sequence—the *Pyar Kiya Toh Darna Kya* song—was reshot in colour, inside a real Sheesh Mahal built using Belgian glass in Bombay's studios with the help of 500 technicians. *Mughal-e-Azam* told the legendary tale of Salim and Anarkali—prince and courtesan, love and defiance—set against the cold grandeur of Emperor Akbar's court. It starred Prithviraj Kapoor, Dilip Kumar, and Madhubala, whose haunting performance as Anarkali remains one of Indian cinema's most beloved. The film's Urdu dialogue was Shakespearean in cadence, its songs—composed by Naushad—timeless in composition, and its visual scale unprecedented.

Upon release, the film became the highest-grossing Indian film of its time, running in theatres for years. But he would never direct another full-length feature. Projects were announced—*Love and God* among them—but none matched the scale or impact of *Mughal-e-Azam,* which stood as both apex and albatross.

K. Asif passed away too soon, leaving behind a slim but storied legacy. In 2004, his magnum opus was digitally remastered and released fully in colour—bringing it to new audiences, where it once again became a hit. That a film could triumph in two different centuries is testimony not just to its grandeur, but to its soul.

BHARAT
KUMAR

Manoj Kumar

For the Love of the Country

(24 July 1937–4 April 2025)

While others made films about India, Manoj Kumar became Bharat himself. Through him, the patriotic film was reborn—not as state propaganda, but as sincere, stirring sentiment. Born Harikishan Giri Goswami in Abbottabad, Manoj Kumar took on his screen name after being inspired by Dilip Kumar's performance in *Shabnam* (1949). He rose to stardom with his striking good looks, intense presence, and an instinct for roles that blended romance with social realism. But it was as a writer-director with a nationalistic vision that he found wide resonance in post-Independence India.

The shift came with *Upkar* (1967). Urged by Prime Minister Shastri's call for *'Jai Jawan, Jai Kisan'*, Kumar crafted a film that honoured the soldier and the farmer in a deeply emotional tale of sacrifice and brotherhood. He played Bharat—a name that would soon become synonymous with his on-screen persona—and the film, with its iconic song *Mere Desh Ki Dharti,* became an instant sensation. *Upkar* was awarded the National Film Award for Best Feature Film on National Integration, and Kumar's image as India's cinematic patriot was sealed. He followed this with *Purab Aur Paschim* (1970), a cross-cultural drama that contrasted Indian values with Western lifestyles. Kumar's character, again named Bharat, wasn't just a person; he was a cultural stand-in, extolling yoga, saris, and tradition while critiquing materialism and rootlessness. *Roti Kapda Aur Makaan* (1974) expanded his canvas to include economic hardship and the betrayal of political promises. The title was the film's thesis—how basic needs are manipulated, corrupted, and denied. He continued this trajectory with *Kranti* (1981), a full-throated epic on India's freedom struggle, starring Dilip Kumar in a comeback role. The film, though theatrically grand, kept Kumar's signature themes alive: sacrifice, national pride, moral clarity.

Manoj Kumar was awarded the Padma Shri and the Dadasaheb Phalke Award in 2016. Though he later retreated from filmmaking, his impact remained etched—especially during every Independence Day and Republic Day, when his songs and scenes found their way back to Indian television screens. In every close-up of a moist eye, every raised salute, every line of trembling conviction, Manoj Kumar reminded India of its better self.

ANNASAHEB

V. Shantaram

The Idealism of Cinema

(18 November 1901–30 October 1990)

If Dadasaheb Phalke gave India its first frame, V. Shantaram gave it movement, melody, and a moral pulse. He took the raw elements of early cinema—myth, drama, silence—and filled them with sound, social reform, and unforgettable spectacle. As one of the first auteurs of Indian cinema, Shantaram directed not only with the camera, but with a conscience.

Shantaram Rajaram Vankudre began his career under the very shadow of Phalke. He joined the Maharashtra Film Company as a teenager, working as a gatekeeper and projectionist before graduating to acting and then direction. His first directorial venture, *Netaji Palkar* (1927), announced a bold visual sensibility and a passion for historical storytelling.

By the '30s, he was making films that were decades ahead of their time. *Amar Jyoti* (1936) featured a female pirate-queen challenging male authority. *Duniya Na Mane* (1937), perhaps his most astonishing film, centred on a young woman forced into marriage with an older man. The film questioned patriarchy, child marriage, and ageism with a sensitivity that modern cinema is still catching up to.

When talkies arrived, Shantaram embraced sound not just for dialogue, but for rhythm. In *Do Aankhen Barah Haath* (1957), perhaps his most enduring work, Shantaram played a prison warden who believes in rehabilitating criminals through hard work and compassion. Based on a real experiment in a Pune prison, the film combined realism with symbolism, ending in heartbreak but affirming hope. It won the Silver Bear at the Berlin Film Festival, and was later honoured with the Golden Globe for Best Foreign Film, making Shantaram one of the first Indian filmmakers to gain global recognition. In *Navrang* (1959), he told the story of a poet in love with his muse—his own wife's alter ego.

V. Shantaram was awarded the Dadasaheb Phalke Award in 1985 and the Padma Vibhushan in 1992 (posthomously). His films span the mythic, the modern, the moral, and the magical. And though his name is often evoked in reverence, his work remains immediate—alive with colour, urgency, and conviction. Across decades, V. Shantaram reflected not just what India was—but what it aspired to become.

Epilogue: Beyond 60

And so the book comes full circle—from Phalke to Shantaram—one amazing filmmaker at a time.

Every list is a door. It opens, yes—but also leaves something behind. To write about 60 filmmakers in a country that produces more than a thousand films a year, across languages, formats, and sensibilities, is to choose with love and to exclude with regret. As you close this book, know that these 60 are not a definitive canon. They are a constellation—a brilliant one—but not the only one. There are other lights in the sky.

We could not include **Sai Paranjpye**, whose *Sparsh* (1980) and *Chashme Buddoor* (1981) gave us stories full of quiet humanity, intelligence, and women with agency and wit. Or **Kundan Shah**, whose *Jaane Bhi Do Yaaro* (1983) remains India's sharpest political satire, a film whose absurdity feels truer with each passing year. We could not find space for **Shivendra Singh Dungarpur**, whose tireless archival work and poetic documentaries like *Celluloid Man* (2012) are a love letter to Indian film history itself.

We had to leave out **T.V. Chandran**, whose Malayalam films explored dislocation, exile, and alienation with rare psychological depth. Nor could we fit **Nagraj Manjule**, whose *Fandry* (2013) and *Sairat* (2016) were not just films but ruptures—narratives that broke into the mainstream with caste, dignity, and defiance at their core. Or **Chaitanya Tamhane**, whose *Court* (2014) is a structural critique of justice told with a stillness so powerful, it silences you long after the credits roll.

We wanted to include **Rima Das**, who directed *Village Rockstars* (2017) almost singlehandedly in Assam and showed that storytelling doesn't need budgets, only honesty. Or **Geetu Mohandas**, whose *Liar's Dice* (2013) and *Moothon* (2019) explored borders both geographic and gendered. And how could one ignore the cinematic audacity of **Lijo Jose Pellissery**, whose Malayalam films—*Ee.Ma.Yau.* (2018), *Jallikattu* (2019), *Churuli* (2021)—feel like hallucinations with a heartbeat?

Some pioneers lived in other corners of the moving image. **Gitanjali Rao**, who brought Indian animation into the art house space with *Bombay Rose* (2019). **Arun Khopkar**, who gave us painterly essays on music and architecture. **K. Hariharan, Tapan Bose, and Suhasini Mulay**, whose documentary and fiction work blurred lines between form and truth. **Revathy,**

Nandita Das, and **Konkona Sen Sharma**, whose turns as directors remind us that powerful women behind the camera are no longer an exception—they're part of the reckoning.

We could not do justice to all the architects of regional cinema—filmmakers like **V.Z. Durai** in Tamil, **Umesh Kulkarni** in Marathi, **Paresh Mokashi, Haobam Paban Kumar, Ravi Jadhav, Jayaraj, Anik Dutta,** or **Kaushik Ganguly**—all of whom carry forward the unique textures of their linguistic and cultural legacies.

Nor could we fit in more documentarians like **Reena Mohan, Nina Sabnani,** or **Rakesh Sharma**, or emerging hybrid filmmakers who navigate between fact and fiction like **Achal Mishra, Shuchi Talati,** or **Varun Grover**—each forging personal languages of cinematic expression.

These omissions are not failures. They are reminders. Reminders that Indian cinema is not a hilltop temple but a vast, crowded, shape-shifting city—sprawling and alive. There are alleys left unexplored, whispers we didn't catch, revolutions still unfolding. But the point was never to map the entire city. The point was to walk with purpose, stop at 60 luminous doorways, and invite you to listen. Because these 60 are not isolated artists. They are entry points. Each one carries within their work the echoes of those who came before and the ripples of those still to come. Dadasaheb Phalke's faith in cinema as national mythology flows into Shantaram's moral theatre, which in turn shapes Manoj Kumar's Bharat and Rakeysh Mehra's awakening youth. Guru Dutt's heartbreak casts its shadow over Raghavan's noir. Ray's gaze lives quietly inside Payal Kapadia's whisper. The lineage is alive.

And it stretches beyond borders. As Indian cinema finds new spaces—film festivals, streaming platforms, OTT anthologies, YouTube shorts, virtual reality—so too do its filmmakers find new voices. Some still speak in metaphors. Others use jump cuts. Some stage musicals in mustard fields. Others leave the frame empty and let the silence speak.

What unites them is not genre, language, or scale. It is intent. It is the refusal to lie. To tell the story that matters, whether it will be seen by a billion or by one.

We hope this book is a beginning. A conversation starter. A bookshelf friend. But most of all, we hope it gives you the same thing these filmmakers gave us: wonder. Wonder at what cinema can do when it chooses not just to entertain, but to mean.

There are many more than 60 amazing filmmakers in India. And somewhere, someone is already writing the next one into being.

Title: One Amazing Filmmaker at a Time
Author: Ena Vismay

ISBN: 978-93-49042-62-9

Published by:
JGS Enterprises Pvt Ltd
Imprint: The Browser

Publisher's Address:
SCO 14-15, FF, Sector 8-C, Chandigarh 160 009
Website: thebrowser.org
Email: service@thebrowser.org

Printed in India

© Layout and Cover Design by 99 beagles
99beagles.com